Seeing the Kingdom

Seeing the Kingdom

Jonathan Mason

seeingthekingdom.com

Kokkoi Limited
2021

Kókkoi

First printing: July 2021

ISBN 978-0-473-58187-9 (softcover)
ISBN 978-0-473-58188-6 (print-on-demand)
ISBN 978-0-473-58189-3 (Epub)
ISBN 978-0-473-58190-9 (Kindle)
Publisher: Kokkoi Limited

Zondervan's Olive Tree app is the best software tool I know for working with Bibles in parallel in various languages, and across all platforms (mine runs across Android, MacOS and iOS). BibleHub's Interlinear Hebrew English web app is likewise a great resource. Liddell and Scott in any version is, in my opinion, the tops; but the Perseus Digital Library online, thanks to Tufts University, makes both LSJ and Middle Liddell enormously accessible. And definitely lighter to carry around.

seeingthekingdom.com

Dedication:

Sarah, ever more

Thanks:

This book, and I, both owe a great deal to other people. In particular, Dr Samantha Callan and my wife, Sarah, helped me, through multiple iterations, to turn the manuscript from a thicket of pointy sticks into something approaching a readable book. Claire Mason worked her everyday wonders with words and images in the final edit, design and layout. To all of you my deepest thanks.

Any mistakes are my own.

Preface: You could blame Kevin

A good and dear friend took me to dinner about three years ago, at a Chinese restaurant down overlooking Plymouth Sound, in South West England. I had already started writing an early version of this book, and was pretty gripped by some of the things I had seen. Kevin got the full force of my enthusiasm, for an hour or more.

He then said a curious thing.

"You need to write a provocation."

I thought I was already being pretty provoking, but he explained what he meant.

In his field - Public Health - it has become common practice when running conferences, to ask one or two people each day to present a 'provocation'. Burnt sticks, eye-poking and tweaked noses are not involved.

Rather, each person presenting a provocation asks for the willing suspension of disbelief, and paints a picture of how things would be if we did things "this way", where "this way" equates to something unthinkable under current rules and conventions. It is an exercise in thinking the unthinkable, of thinking outside the box.

Doubtless on some occasions it goes no further. But there are, of course, those occasions when, having surveyed the newly opened horizons offered by this unthinkable thought, people look at one another and ask: "why exactly can't we do this?" And so progress is made.

I hope you won't be provoked in the useless sense of that word; surely there are enough things to make us all shout at the radio, TV or laptop, without adding additional stressors. But I will be pleased if you get as far as asking, "well, if we allowed for a moment that some of what this person is saying might be true, what difference would it make?"

Because, as it happens, I think we as the Church are overdue to reclaim some very important territory that has been ours all along; only we allowed ourselves to be talked out of it, somewhere along the line.

If this doesn't work for you, my apologies, and the blame is all mine. But if we turn a light or two on for you, you might want to thank Kevin.

I certainly do.

Prologue: Why did I write this book, and why would you read it?

The first time I wrote a book, I was holding a copy in my hands, fresh from the printers, just 23 days after I wrote the opening sentence. This book has been a little longer in the making.

My objective is, I think, a simple one. I want to write something which helps brothers and sisters see things they may have been missing, concerning the Kingdom of God. That is a practical objective; I believe that when you see these things clearly, it changes the way you experience the Kingdom, and for the better.

The reason for focusing on the Kingdom of God is simple: the most important difference between the Old Testament and the New **is** the Kingdom of God; Jesus' preaching and teaching from start to finish was focused on The Kingdom; and yet we have marginalised the Kingdom as a rather "knowing" way of saying 'The Church'; which it most certainly is not, at least not in Jesus' mouth.

In a perfect world, I would simply share these passages and my reading of them, and let everyone draw their own conclusions. I am, however, advised that I need to say something about why I think I can and should challenge well-accepted readings of Scripture; and secondly, what the meta-narrative is. In other words, is there a thread that binds together these chapters, not to mention the biblical passages they cover?

Translation

I have been collecting mistranslations - oddly persistent ones - in the New Testament as long as I can remember, certainly for the last 40 years. What I mean by "a mistranslation" in this context is somewhere that the plain meaning of the Greek has been overridden and the meaning changed in the English. Doubtless many will say, "yes but, translation is all about context and culture and so on", to which I would answer, "possibly, but far less often than you might think."

I am not generally talking about debatable choices between possible meanings of words. I am talking about ignoring what a word "means", when it makes perfect sense in context, and instead, making it say something else.

In fact, it didn't take me long to work out that, in the cases I am talking about, the common factor leading to what I am calling "mistranslation" was not the culture of first Century Judaea, but rather the Church culture of the translators, themselves.

It is hardly surprising; common sense suggests that when we read something which doesn't compute for us, we are likely to say "well it can't mean that, so let's try to reshape it until it does make sense".

But what if it **does** mean 'that' (whatever 'that' is)?

Let me give you a simple example. Colossians 4:17 in the NIV reads as follows:

Tell Archippus: "See to it that you complete the ministry you have received in the Lord."

Most of the modern English translations have something similar. The King James and many others have, or have something close to, "Take heed to the ministry which thou hast received in the Lord, that thou fulfil it." Meanwhile, you are probably trying to remember when you last heard a sermon on Colossians 4:17; it probably never happened, so what is the problem, here?

Only this: the Greek doesn't say what the NIV says.

Anyone with a good, basic grasp of Greek (and, preferably, no access to an English version of the passage to mimic unconsciously) should be able to render this correctly:

καὶ εἴπατε Ἀρχίππῳ· Βλέπε τὴν διακονίαν ἣν παρέλαβες ἐν κυρίῳ, ἵνα αὐτὴν πληροῖς.

It means, quite simply and word for word:

And say to Archippus, "See the assignment which you have received in the Lord, in order that you may fulfil it."

The difference, once you see it, is stark. The NIV is assuming Archippus has a ministry he is already aware of, and urges him to focus on that so that he completes it. Paul, based on the Greek of the this verse, makes no such assumption - he instead exhorts Archippus to **see** what assignment he has received in the Lord - because until he sees it, how can he possibly fulfil it?

In passing, my use of 'assignment' rather than 'ministry' is deliberate. διακονίαν means 'the service of a servant'; we have christianised this into a thing called 'ministry', which is freighted with meaning, little of which was likely in Paul's mind. 'Assignment' is a good word which captures the idea of 'meaningful work to do for a superior', without loading it with religious baggage.

But back to the main point - why did the NIV translators and others change the simple and apparently inoffensive meaning of Colossians 4:17?

The conclusion I arrived at 40 years ago, still seems likely to me: namely that this dates back to a time (not so very long ago) when you only had a 'ministry' if you also had a back-to-front collar, or other distinguishing feature suggesting that ordination had occurred. From **that** context and perspective, the idea that someone could have a ministry and **not know it** is plainly absurd.

"You must surely remember whether you went through Theological training or not. You would remember meeting the Bishop, surely? Tall man in purple, wearing a mitre?"

So, if what I suspect is true, this illustrates what happens when Scripture says something which doesn't fit into **our** mental space.

We say, "it can't mean that"; and in this case we make "see" into an idiomatic statement - see to it, take heed - which then changes Archippus' relationship to his assignment as well. We end up with an anodyne exhortation ("keep going, old chap...") rather than the metaphorical, almost literal, one of the original - "come on Archippus, **see your assignment**".

In doing so, we miss a truth, which Paul at least knew and understood. Citizens of the Kingdom have assignments from the Lord; but they need to see their assignment and understand what it is that God is asking them to do, if they are ever to fulfil it.

This is actually a valuable insight when, for example, you are discipling believers, young or old. "You need to learn what God is teaching you here, because He already has places for you to go and stuff for you to accomplish; and you need to learn how to hear what God is telling you..."

Let me share another Pauline example, where I think I can nail down *who* made the change, if not *why*.

Philippians 4:11 in the NIV says:

*I am not saying this because I am in need, for I have learned **to be content** whatever the circumstances.* (my emphasis)

What the Greek says is once again quite different:

οὐχ ὅτι καθ' ὑστέρησιν λέγω, ἐγὼ γὰρ ἔμαθον ἐν οἷς εἰμι

αὐτάρκης εἶναι·

which means

> I am not saying this through lack, for I have learned, in
> whatever [situation] I am to be **self-sufficient**.

Personally, I can say that seeing that word αὐτάρκης was a complete
game-changer for me. I knew the word, not least because it has
passed into modern political economy with meaning unchanged.
Autarky - self-sufficiency, particularly in the means to wage war
- was a key pillar of the Third Reich, for example. I just couldn't
immediately get my head around what it meant **in this context**, but
I knew that God had just flipped my dinghy upside down.

It made sense, of course - Paul was always more likely to walk
through a wall than "accept adverse circumstances with a quiet
serenity" - but it was more than that. Self-sufficient was unlikely to
mean "I just do my own thing", but it certainly flagged the fact that
Paul had his active part to play in a way that "contented" simply
didn't suggest or even permit.

So how did we ever get to 'contented'? I can't tell you why, but I
can say who.

Jerome, in the Vulgate, translated αὐτάρκης as *'sum sufficiens esse'*;
Luther translated it as *'mir genügen zu lassen'*; Wycliffe (whoever he
or they really were) said *"for Y haue lerud to be sufficient in whiche
thingis Y am"*. So up to that point, translators into Latin, German
and English are preserving the meaning of αὐτάρκης, with accuracy.
And then comes William Tyndale, who translates the phrase as *"For
I have learned in whatsoever estate I am therewith to be content."*

We know Tyndale was influential, because every single English
translation since Tyndale (at least all the ones I have checked, which
is very many), follows Tyndale and says 'content' or 'contented'.

And this - translators following one another's lead, rather than translating the Greek - happens far more than it should.

And here is the tricky bit: Dictionaries of NT Greek get infected by the decisions translators make, in a way that happens far less with general Greek Dictionaries. For this reason I would always use Liddell and Scott's Greek-English Lexicon in preference to the other dictionaries at my disposal, if I am looking at **meaning**; the others have their uses, but mostly for citations of where a word or phrase occurs in the NT or Patristic Texts. I don't believe they can be trusted as a guide to meaning or lexical accuracy, precisely because they tend to record the decisions of prior translators, and therefore act as theological and cultural echo chambers of a later age, rather than authoritative guides to usage in NT times.

When Liddell and Scott pick up these usages by the translators - and they do - you can at least see them coming; the word will be cited with a meaning distinct from its usual meaning, and will be so cited in reference to a NT passage, meaning you can evaluate what has happened critically. (And sometimes the translation will be perfectly reasonable; but my point is, in this context, with a mix of biblical and non-biblical usage, you at least have some chance to judge what has happened; something you can't often do with the specifically NT Dictionaries).

So don't be surprised if your Dictionary of NT Greek tells you that αὐτάρκης **does** mean 'contented'. What they really mean is that Tyndale decided αὐτάρκης must mean 'content' in the context of Philippians 4, and every translator since was happy to follow Tyndale; but I would simply argue that he, and therefore they, were wrong.

So why did Tyndale do it? Well, he lived in perilous times, and had nailed his flag to Luther's flagpole. It is possible he found "self-sufficient" to be at odds with the Lutheran "only faith" (*sola fide*) doctrine. He was also a trained humanist, and it is possible he thought that Paul was deliberately referencing Stoic thought as a virtue.[1]

We can't know the 'why' of Tyndale's shift from "self-sufficient" to "contented", but it seems ill-judged. Presumably he didn't understand the extent to which he was giving a badly wrong steer to five hundred years-worth of believers coming after him. Tyndale lived in pretty adverse circumstances himself; so perhaps his rendering of Philippians 4:11 gave him solace. But being contented with your adverse circumstances is definitely **not** a Kingdom virtue, as we shall discover.

I could go on - and I will, but will do so in the context of the passages we are going to look at. Let me underline that this is not *at all* a book about "your Bible is translated all wrong". Mostly if there are translation issues, they are just making it **harder to see what is there**. The real problem is that most of us don't seem to be seeing the Kingdom, even when it is clear and plain and in broad daylight.

I would have preferred not to have had to raise the translation issue; but if I simply start saying in the text, "this means x, not y as your version of the Bible may say", someone is going to ask *"by what right or authority…"*

I don't plan to answer that exactly (this is a provocation, remember), but I wouldn't be doing this if I wasn't confident that I have a valid point of view on all this, both in terms of "what texts mean" and more especially on "how to read texts in their historical context".

---

[1] *A very unlikely idea, even though generations of commentators since Tyndale have felt they had to make the connection - what is clear is that Paul ironically references the mystery religions in his statement "I have been initiated into the secret…"; but no one seems to be suggesting the Paul is holding up the Cult of Mithras as a role model. So why try to make Paul a follower of Zeno (or more weirdly, a disciple of Epictetus, who, as far as we know, was born when Paul was already in mid-career) as well as of Jesus?*

The Meta-Narrative

My original plan was simply to examine a number of passages and let the results speak for themselves. Wiser heads than mine insist that this was a bad plan. However, I confess to some reluctance in stating what the over-arching narrative is here, and for a simple enough reason.

Jesus proclaimed His message openly and clearly, and yet veiled from casual view - especially through His use of parables. I think He makes it perfectly clear that no one understands His words unless they have been given the key by the Father; the corollary of this is that **anyone** can ask the Father for wisdom and therefore receive the key to what He says.

Without the key, we will not understand. Nicodemus, in John 3, thought he was affirming Jesus by making his grand statement that His (i.e. Jesus') works showed that God was with Him; Jesus replied that Nicodemus didn't understand at all (i.e. his 'gracious' comment was just plain wrong) because he couldn't see the Kingdom, and wouldn't until he experienced a new birth; and Nicodemus struggled to understand that idea, also.

Jesus also has no difficulty at all in misdirecting His hearers, to prevent revelation being understood prematurely. Take for example, His statement in John 2:19 "Destroy this temple, and I will raise it again in three days." Funnily enough, all three of the synoptic Gospels have the hostile witnesses quoting this statement at Jesus' arraignment, even though only John presents the saying in its original context.

Because His authority was being questioned on account of His clearing of the Temple (in John 2), all His hearers - including the disciples - assume He is talking about the Temple of Herod. Only with hindsight, were they able correctly to interpret His words as referring to the 'Temple' of His body. Jesus knows perfectly well that they have misunderstood Him, and yet is happy to leave things that way.

Which makes it a very serious business to say what Jesus meant. It seems to me that most error - and most mistranslation - begins with someone saying "aha, this is what it all means", and off we go down another alley of half-truth. Half truth won't help us. And yet, of course, it is very hard to teach anyone anything without at some point nailing something to the mast; I am just saying, the warning in James 3:1 (*"Not many of you should become teachers, my fellow believers, because you know that we who teach will be judged more strictly"*) is a warning I take to heart.

I am, however, compelled...

My simple aim therefore, is to look at specific passages and try to clear accumulated misunderstandings away. As it happens, I spent yesterday afternoon, clearing wisteria from a small patch of New Zealand bush. The wisteria was beautiful when it graced the porch of our family home in Auckland; but my mother thought it would thrive out on the farm. And it did, but not in a good way. I lost count of how many stems I cut yesterday in a patch no more than 10 metres by 3, but it was somewhere well north of 350. I arrived in time for some of the trees, but others were already dead on their feet, well strangled by the vines.

This work has been a lot like clearing wisteria; only, of course, the Word of God resists every attempt to strangle it, and it cannot be killed. In all truth, I have been hungering after this Kingdom since I first caught a glimpse of it, aged 14. The problem was that I couldn't "get" it until someone did two things for me: showed me the narrative of Scripture as a coherent whole; and modelled how to walk out the Kingdom in reality. And that - how to walk it out - was what I had been looking for my whole life.

This present work, I reiterate, is just a provocation. People walking out the Kingdom and teaching others to do likewise are what we really need. Good field manuals, too.

That being said, **let me share the threads which I believe tie the whole together**. These threads are absolutely present in every single one of the passages we are going to look at. All my clearing away 'the wisteria of misperception' would count for nothing without these themes of the Kingdom. Seeing and articulating them was done by others, so I claim no credit; I just affirm them as both scriptural and central to the teaching of Jesus.

First and foremost, **the Kingdom of God** is a Kingdom and therefore **operates on the basis of law**. Law establishes **how things work** in any domain, and the Kingdom of God (or "of the Heavens") is no different.[1]

You can actually identify many (but not all) of the points where Jesus is teaching Kingdom law, because He introduces it by saying something like "truly I tell you" or "very truly I say to you" (in the Greek of the synoptics, either ἀμὴν λέγω ὑμῖν or λέγω δὲ ὑμῖν ἀληθῶς; and in John ἀμὴν ἀμὴν λέγω ὑμῖν). If we wanted to be colloquial, we might say, "pin your ears back, you need to hear this"; or possibly even just, "are you getting this? 'Cause you better had... "

In the passage we call the Great Commission in Matthew 28, Jesus instructs the disciples to make disciples, baptising them and instructing them to 'keep as commandments' all that Jesus has commanded them. In the Greek that is τηρεῖν πάντα ὅσα ἐνετειλάμην ὑμῖν, the last part of which carries the sense not only of "what I have commanded you" but also of "what I have legally

---

[1] *A quick warning. It is best not to make judgements based on word association. If you find yourself reacting to the word "law" and wanting to quote Romans back at me, please quote it all, including, for example, Romans 3:27 "Because of what law? The law that requires works? No, because of the law that requires faith"; and Romans 8:2 "the law of the Spirit who gives life". In other words, not all law is the Law of Moses.*

authorised you to enact". At the point where Jesus has completed His assignment, He summarises His actions and their future application using the language of legal frameworks.

And there is a reason why Kingdom law matters so much.

God is not deciding outcomes on a case by case basis. He does not say 'yes' to me, 'no' to you, and 'maybe - let me get back to you on that' to your Aunt Cassie. He does not say this one can be healed, and this one will learn more if they suffer or die. He does not take babies because Heaven is short on flowers. And I shouldn't have to write this paragraph, because God has made His purpose plain, in Jesus. He has already committed Himself to give you everything you could possibly need, healing, provision, forgiveness, purpose; and He **does not** "give and take away". If you insist on getting your theology from Job's outbursts when he was in the middle of his self-righteous tantrum against God, then of course you will end up confused.

So a second, vital thread in our meta-narrative is that **God is good**; His intention towards us is only good; and if He is wrathful, that wrath is not directed at us. If that seems shocking, we will address this further. But you can say to anyone you meet, with absolute truth, "God is not mad at you." It is one of the most healing, saving truths there is.

Which brings us to two other threads: one, that **we have an enemy** who is playing for time with human shields, and for whom, perverting mankind's view of God is the most fruitful strategy; and two, that **you and I have authority on earth**.

What do I mean? Satan was already under sentence of destruction for rebellion when God put Adam and Eve in the Garden. He knew that if he could bring them in to his own rebellion - if he could get them to obey him, while simultaneously disobeying God, then God would not be able to execute judgement on him (Satan) without also destroying His beloved children, Adam and Eve. Human shields; Saddam Hussein didn't invent the idea, not by a long chalk.

Satan operated on them by selling them the idea that God was trying to hold them back. I won't spoil the suspense, but I would be surprised if many of us can read all the chapters of this book without somewhere coming to a realisation that we also have been sold some lie or other, and, worse, that we thought it was sound doctrine.

What about my claim that **we** have authority? Surely Jesus has all authority in heaven and on the earth? Yes, and we will look at what authority actually means; but Adam and Eve were given *delegated* authority on earth, and although Satan may have stolen their crowns, every human being still has that delegated authority.

That doesn't mean that exercising this authority while you are separated from God and subject to your number one enemy will end well for you; but you do have authority. It is what makes you so dangerous - especially to yourself. Bring that authority back under the authority of Him who is King of Kings and Lord of Lords, and **you become dangerous in the way God always meant you to be**; one who can take ground back and deny it to the enemy.

I won't give an exhaustive list of all the themes we will cover beyond those three above, but one needs to be mentioned: **money**. Why is it, I wonder, that for a sizeable portion of the church, we can only talk about money if first we make it clear that we aren't preaching **prosperity**. Which is a little weird, given how much God has said about His intention to make His people notoriously prosperous (notoriously, in that all the nations will see that prosperity and declare us blessed by God).

If ever Satan has sold us all a lie, it is here. In the earth realm, which is the only place in which we can pursue the assignment God has given us, nothing happens without money or its proxies. This is actually true, whether you like it or not. Faith missions? Nothing ever happened in a faith mission without money. Volunteers are not free - someone has to pay to feed and clothe and house them.

If you are devoted to God's Kingdom, and God can tap you on the shoulder any time and say, "I need $20 million to get this assignment done..."; at what point would you have too much money? Surely the question answers itself. And yet people say to me, "yes, we should be blessed, but not too much." I presume that means we should pursue the assignment God gives us, and support the assignments of others, but also - not too much. I don't think we mean what we say.

Now notice I didn't say that money alone gets things done, but I did say that nothing happens without it. I don't want to pre-empt what our passages will teach us, but we need to understand what money is. If you think that, if I should happen to buy a car - let's make it a Lamborghini, for shock value - then starving children will go without dinner, you have failed to understand what the economy is. Actually, when I buy a Lambo, many workers in Bologna are able to put food on the table; their action in buying that food means, in turn, that shopkeepers can feed their families, and farmers can buy seed and shirts and school books for their children and so on. The Church's determined pursuit of poverty is one of the strangest features of our story, and only tends to misery for the many.

The truth is, you can't draw a boundary between "cars a Christian might own" and "cars no Christian should own" without becoming exactly what the Pharisees were; guilty of promoting your own prejudices in the guise of holy commandments. Nor is such a question even important. The real issue is that, if there is an assignment you should be seeing and completing (Colossians 4:17), how will you do so without access to provision? And provision is mostly just money or things that stand for money.

Of all the threads of this meta-narrative, money seems to demand the most justification, not least because it produces the strangest responses from believers one would expect to know better.

So I would simply observe that the most fiercely-contested truths (biblical truths, contested by the enemy) point to vulnerabilities in his (Satan's) position.

Satan already accepts he can't keep you out of heaven. But his maintenance of his wretched kingdom here depends on you not knowing the rights you have in the Kingdom of The Heavens; that the favour of God is upon you; that Satan has no power, only a line of deception to feed you; and that you have, not only authority, but also the provision that accompanies authority (the Greek word ἐξουσία covers both). Satan would really like you to remain ignorant of all that.

For those with an enquiring turn of mind, let me seed this thought: by taking back-bearings from areas and subjects which are the most highly-contested by the enemy, we may get some clues as to what the ruler of this world is most frightened that we might find out. (Just don't get too clever about it; the important thing is that we keep going back to Jesus and His words.)

And if you really want to understand why I have persevered and written this book:

Damned wisteria! Cut it off at the roots, poison the stump - and set the garden free...

Chapter One: Scattering Seed

"Listen! A farmer went out to sow his seed. As he was scattering the seed, some fell along the path, and the birds came and ate it up. Some fell on rocky places, where it did not have much soil. It sprang up quickly, because the soil was shallow. But when the sun came up, the plants were scorched, and they withered because they had no root. Other seed fell among thorns, which grew up and choked the plants, so that they did not bear grain. Still other seed fell on good soil. It came up, grew and produced a crop, some multiplying thirty, some sixty, some a hundred times."

Mark 4:3-8, NIV

What are we looking at here?

Jesus told this deceptively simple parable to the crowd. As a story, it couldn't be more straightforward: a man goes out sowing seed, but it is where the seed lands which determines the outcome.

The disciples, however, didn't understand **why** Jesus told the story, and came to Him afterwards, privately, and asked how they should be interpreting the parable. Before explaining it to them, He informed them that if they don't understand this parable, they will be hard pressed to understand any of the others. Which is rather alarming for the disciples, but also an important flag for us: this might be, in some way, at the core of Jesus' message to us.

He then interpreted the parable for them: the seed sown is the Word, the place where it lands is different kinds of people, **based on how they respond** to the Word.

Luke in his version indicates that this response is based upon **their hearts**, and that the soil is their hearts ("takes away the word from their hearts" in Luke 8:12, and "But the seed on good soil stands for those with a noble and good heart," in Luke 8:15). That *seed* = *word* and *soil* = *heart* template is therefore probably a good one to internalise.

So far so good.

It would be possible to read more into the story than is indicated by the explanation Jesus gave; specifically some kind of success metric. Jesus has, after all, already said that "good-soil" type people reproduce the seed that was sown, thirty-, sixty- or a hundred-fold. But there is another metric implied in the story.

To illustrate, let me ask you: according to Jesus, what percentage of people have "good soil"-type hearts?

Because we are following the **structure** of the story, rather than necessarily living in the same **context**, our calculation could easily go like this: "there are four types of soil, three resistant in some way to the Word of God, and one which is open to the Word of God. So that gives us roughly 3/4 or 75% who we can expect to resist the Word, and at most 1/4 or 25% who are open."

And it isn't too much of a stretch to go a step further and say "So we shouldn't be bothered or surprised when most people won't listen." Which is a sermon I have heard, and more than once.

What's wrong with this picture?

If we have followed the "25% are open" chain of reasoning, then clearly we are thinking of four roughly equal-sized categories of people described in the parable. Jesus however tells a story in which the categories, **in context**, cannot under any circumstances be equal in size to one another.

If that is so, then the Parable of the Sower is saying just about the opposite of the position I described above (that most people will reject the Word they hear). The implication of what Jesus says is that a much larger percentage of people will have open, receptive hearts than the "maybe a quarter" which we have been thinking.

What should we be seeing instead?

Jesus was speaking to people in Galilee, by the Lake. Even those who lived in the town of Capernaum were not far removed from agricultural life, at least not in the way that perhaps most of us are. So they understood the picture that Jesus was painting.

But you can too: all you need to do is visualise the story and you will see the point.

"The sower went out to sow." Visualise a ploughed field. Even if you have never walked across a ploughed field, you likely drew one when you were in kindergarten, along with a tractor, some cabbages and a smiling farmer (who was probably wearing a ridiculously large hat).

Make the ploughed field as big or as small as you like. It is unlikely to be smaller than a tennis court though; this is a commercial field, not a cottage garden.

Now Jesus **could** have said "a farmer went out to sow" (which is in fact what the NIV rather inaccurately says), but He used a very specific term and said "the one who sows", rather than "a farmer" (which would be γεωργός). This is most probably referencing a professional who sows fields for all the farmers in an area. It could be that one of the farmhands is always asked to do all the sowing and so is called "the sower"; but either way, the implication is that he actually knows what he is doing. (Although even an inexpert farmer would be bound to do a better job than the one we have been picturing.)

So now picture this knowledgable, skilful sower, walking up and down the field you have visualised, reaching into the seed bag slung around one shoulder and broadcasting his seed, with long sweeps of his arm.

Along one side of the field you have visualised, there is a path. It hasn't been ploughed up, it is beaten hard by the passage of many feet and any seed that lands on it just bounces and sits on the surface. Birds eat it.

At both ends of the field, there is a rocky headland (a technical ploughing term for the area immediately past where the animal(s) and plough make their turn) where all the rocks from the field have been carried. Any seed that falls amongst the rocks may make a dash for survival, but is likely to shrivel in the sun for want of accessible soil.

Down the side of the field furthest from the path, there is unploughed ground. Being unploughed means it is home to all sorts of things - probably some self-seeded wheat from previous crops, but plenty of weeds as well. Any seed that falls in here will get to grow up, but is unlikely to be able to produce seeds in its desperate fight for survival with the competing weeds.

So you have visualised the field, and its adjoining territories, and you are watching the sower walk up and down, sowing his seed. His aim, of course, is to sow his seed into the good, ploughed soil.

So: *what percentage of his seed lands in the good ploughed soil?*

Of course there isn't "a right answer", and Jesus wasn't teaching percentages. But the 25% we were talking about earlier is clearly wrong. So what did you say?

For what it is worth, if your answer is only 90%, I doubt our sower will ever work in this town again. I suspect that wasting 10% of the precious seed would not make him popular or valued. Some wastage is inevitable but the success rate probably needs to be in the 97-98% range for our sower to be invited back.

25% success rate and he doesn't even make it home tonight. He is strung up by his sandals, as a warning to others.

What does this mean?

As I just said, Jesus wasn't teaching about percentage receptivity (at least not directly); but He was painting a picture. The heart of the picture is about fruitfulness - seed reproducing thirty-, sixty- and a hundred-fold. Most of the seed ends up in the good soil and being fruitful. The warning of the parable is "don't miss out on what everybody else is going to experience, just because you have a hard heart, enthusiasm without depth or too many other cares and concerns".

This would have been immediately clear to those listening to Jesus, because He was accessing a scene from common experience; and it should be clear to us, also, the moment we actually allow the words which we have been hearing all these years to form the picture they really carry.

Maybe that is why in Mark 4:24, Jesus says to the disciples, Βλέπετε τί ἀκούετε (*blepete ti akouete* - see what you hear). We tend to make the first part (Βλέπετε, see) into a metaphorical statement - "watch out", or "take heed". But in context, I think Jesus is warning His disciples to allow "what they hear" (from Him) to turn into "the picture they see". Having the right picture is going to be key to "getting it"; and, for example, leads to being able to use the right measure to measure things with. (Mark 4:25)

And for what it is worth, I think most of the occasions when the disciples react with alarm, fear or dismay to something Jesus has said can be explained by their responding to the *words*, instead of the *picture* the words should be painting for them. Acquiring the same habit - of actually seeing the picture the words create, rather than just reacting to words we haven't properly understood - is going to help us to see the Kingdom for ourselves.

What does this mean for me?

This is a fairly gentle example of the phenomenon we are addressing in this book, namely of ways we might have been misreading or misperceiving the message Jesus brings concerning the Kingdom of God. At this early stage of this journey, I wouldn't be surprised if you were somewhat sceptical about where this is going, and that is fine - but please stay with me on this journey, at least until you have seen a little more.

My own experience has been that things I have accepted uncritically, and maybe for many years, can be pretty hard to let go of. Unfortunately, to really see the Kingdom, some "letting go" of treasured certainties is almost inevitable - just as it was to those who followed Jesus during His ministry on earth. For now, it will be enough if we can agree that the Parable of the Sower does **not** predict a high rejection rate for the Good News.

If you can go a step further and agree that the Parable suggests that sowing God's word into hearts is meant to have a very high response rate, with great fruitfulness, then that is a result!

As a bonus fact: a year or two back, I made a study of academic literature on the cultivation of wheat around the world, because I was interested in yield rates, to see how wheat fields under modern cultivation compared with what Jesus said.

Density of sowing varies hugely, depending on rainfall and soil type. So in different places, someone might sow 45 kilograms of seed per hectare, and somewhere else it might be 80 kilograms.

But what was very consistent was average yield. Germination rates (i.e. all the way through to a plant that bears grain) are a very consistent 80%; in other words, 4 out of every 5 grains you sow will grow to be a cropping plant.

And although the number of ears per plant varies, the average is 5 ears, each of 22 corns (grains). That means the average plant has 110 grains of wheat at harvest time, and 80% of what was sown grows to harvest, so 110 x 80% = a return on the number of seeds you sowed of 88 times. Factoring in ancient challenges such as pests without pesticides etc, '30-fold, 60-fold and 100-fold" is definitely in the same ball park.

But all of this leads us to another question: where on earth did we get the idea that the Parable of the Sower is a "salvation parable"?

Jesus doesn't say it is about people responding to the Good News and entering the Kingdom (although presumably it includes that). He says it is about the response of hearts to the Word of God. We surely aren't saying that salvation is the only reason God's Word comes our way? Or maybe we are; but that isn't what Jesus believed.

Let's just walk back over that field again.

Have you ever read something in the Bible or heard God speak to you in some way which struck you forcibly? It is that sense of being stopped in your tracks and saying "Wow, what was that?"

This applies whether you were a believer at the time or not. And don't think for a moment that the only thing God speaks to those who aren't yet believers is some variation of "repent or be destroyed". I know so many people who heard God speak before they really knew Him or even understood who He is, and what they heard was almost always some promise about their future. (Just like Abram did in Genesis 12, huh?)

But here's the question: after you heard that Word, what happened next?

I know the answer for myself: way too often, I simply stop in the moment, say "that is very encouraging", occasionally write it down - and then forget it ever happened. Which would put me somewhere in soil number two.

So what is the outcome when God speaks His Word into your heart? It is meant to land in good, receptive soil. Is that what happens? Or does it go 'ping!' as it ricochets off the hard packed earth, and gets snatched away by any passing demon? Does it shoot up quickly and die even faster? Does it get throttled by all of your cares and concerns?

Well, hopefully not. Jesus told this parable with the expectation that most of what is sown, lands in good soil and produces a return 30-fold, 60-fold or a 100-fold. My earlier bonus fact simply confirms this is a realistic expectation for wheat; and Jesus is saying the seed of God's word, sown into your heart, should be at least that fruitful, too!

So what would that look like?

God gives you a word about a serious health issue (for example), and because you receive it with a good heart and take that word seriously and allow it to grow up in your heart, the day comes when you know that you know that you know that "I am healed". And that is not because your circumstances have changed (yet) but because "by His stripes we are healed" means you are already healed. Your healing is a historic fact, so you receive it as such. And sometime after that, you wake up one day and the illness has disappeared.

For myself it was chronic bacterial chest infections (as an adult, I have averaged 6 or 7 courses of antibiotics per year). My doctor in Singapore even asked if I had tried prayer, and I said "yes, as a matter of fact." But then God challenged me with something I had seen in scripture some years earlier: that Jesus never once prayed for a sick person to be healed, nor did He tell His Disciples to do so.

He, and they, simply healed people. This suggested to me that healing wasn't about asking ("O Lord, please heal me") but rather about enforcing Kingdom law ("You're healed"). And then I started listening to the testimonies of others in our Church who had been healed by allowing the word of God to get into their hearts and then grow into a full grown plant there.

I finally got serious with that word and others like it, tended them, and with perseverance brought forth a harvest - which meant getting to the point that every time a chest infection tried starting, I was able to simply refuse it, and tell it that it had no place or authority in my body. Each time this happened, it disappeared more quickly, and I now haven't been to the doctor for a chest infection in over 6 years. I have no objection to doctors, but I am much more interested in allowing my microbiome to recover from 50 years of antibiotics.

If chest infections aren't a big enough deal for you, I have friends who have had enormous tumours disappear, been healed of final stage cancer and much more. And what do you think happens when someone who is visibly misshapen with a tumour, or who has been given 4 days to live, is suddenly back to normal and popping into the shop to buy groceries?

If you guess that other people who have health issues start seeing there is an answer to their problem and have the same experience of God's covenant of healing, you would be right.

You see one seed goes into good soil and produces a living fruitful plant - and that is **your** healing. But it bears fruit, thirty, sixty and one hundred fold, and that is a whole lot of people receiving their healing.

That is the pattern Jesus is teaching us in this parable. Whatever the Word is that you receive, I can guarantee it is never meant just to encourage you. It should encourage you; but if all you do is say "that's nice" and trundle on, you are somewhere between soil two and soil three.

God gives you a Word because you need to change, and that Word is your means to see and to achieve that change. It could be about your health, turning around your finances, saving your marriage, restoring your family, anything.

So take it seriously, work with it, allow it to change you and bring forth your answer. But in the Kingdom, when you receive your answer, that means a whole lot of other people can see and receive their answer too.

And that is the Parable of the Sower.

So, where to next?

In the next Chapter we are going to look at another passage which appears to illuminate "response rates" for us, but which may in fact be telling the opposite story to the one we thought we heard; the Wedding Banquet of the King's Son.

Chapter Two: Party Invite

"The kingdom of heaven is like a king who prepared a wedding banquet for his son. He sent his servants to those who had been invited to the banquet to tell them to come, but they refused to come.

"Then he sent some more servants and said, 'Tell those who have been invited that I have prepared my dinner: My oxen and fattened cattle have been butchered, and everything is ready. Come to the wedding banquet.'

"But they paid no attention and went off—one to his field, another to his business. The rest seized his servants, mistreated them and killed them. The king was enraged. He sent his army and destroyed those murderers and burned their city.

"Then he said to his servants, 'The wedding banquet is ready, but those I invited did not deserve to come. So go to the street corners and invite to the banquet anyone you find.' So the servants went out into the streets and gathered all the people they could find, the bad as well as the good, and the wedding hall was filled with guests.

"But when the king came in to see the guests, he noticed a man there who was not wearing wedding clothes. He asked, 'How did you get in here without wedding clothes, friend?' The man was speechless.

"Then the king told the attendants, 'Tie him hand and foot, and throw him outside, into the darkness, where there will be weeping and gnashing of teeth.'

"For many are invited, but few are chosen."

Matthew 22:2-14, NIV

What are we looking at here?

This parable certainly looks a lot like a tale of multiple rejections.

The invited guests reject the King's invitation; the King destroys the invited guests. His servants bring in people off the street; the King rejects street people who are improperly dressed.

And there is a strange comfort in the final words of the parable, for those of us wounded by the apparent lack of response to the Gospel. We have worked our hearts out, but have concluded that people can't possibly want to know about the Gospel, or else we would see more of them flocking to our churches.

See: 'many are called but few are chosen'. We have done our best, and people turn up from time to time, but so many of them never really belonged here.

What's wrong with this picture?

What appears to be an open-and-shut case, has at least one very curious feature. That is, that the final sentence of the parable as we have it in English **doesn't actually match** the rest of the parable.

We may be reading that sentence as if it sums up the parable, when actually it stands in opposition to what comes before. Something is not quite right. The parable itself is about "there is lots of room and plenty of people at this banquet", and not at all about "few are chosen"!

What should we be seeing instead?

Firstly it is worth noting that - despite assertions to the contrary - parables can make more than one point.

Anytime Jesus says anything, we need to be paying attention all the time, especially when He tells stories, because He is quite capable of driving His main point down-range, as it were - and then clipping us around the ear on His follow-through.

This Parable definitely has several threads. And here is the central one: responding to the Kingdom of God is as simple as turning up for an amazing party.

Which is not what you might conclude from every Sunday service you have ever attended.

The picture in the New Testament is actually quite simple. Both Acts 2 and Romans 10 quote the promise of Joel 2:32 "anyone whoever that calls on the Name of Yahweh shall be saved".

The invitation Jesus extends most often is "come, follow me."

And in our current parable we find this:

So the servants went out into the streets and gathered all the people they could find, the bad as well as the good, and the wedding hall was filled with guests.

So the Kingdom of God is like a party - a wedding banquet, put on by the King for His Son - and entering the Kingdom of God requires that when you are invited, **you turn up**. (The invited guests didn't; the street people did.)

It really doesn't seem that complicated; but there is an action required. Joel 2 says "anyone whoever that calls on the Name of Yahweh"; in Matthew 22 you just respond to the invitation and turn up.

So that is the core story in Matthew 22:2-14. It is not a story that matches what you have been thinking was meant by "for many are invited, but few are chosen." The hall is full of street people, "**bad** as well as good" and the King happily walks among them.

But what about the other threads?

The wedding hall is **filled** with guests. And yes, **one** of them is turfed out - but we will come to that in a minute. Let's back up first.

There was a group of people who were originally invited by the King, who ended up being slaughtered. What is this about?

Is it a warning to the leaders of the Jewish nation? Yes, clearly. If anyone is invited to Yahweh's wedding feast, clearly it should be them. Does it mean that they - the leaders of the Jews - should all be slaughtered? Clearly no.

Jesus' intention is to use a story to expose the peril the leaders of the nation are putting themselves in. In the parable, no one is killed for refusing to come the first or second time. Those who went off to their field or their business are not killed.

But in the story, which is a story about an earthly King, those who seize and murder the King's messengers have the King's vengeance to contend with; any King would do the same. Jesus is simply making an appeal to their common sense, about the consequences of refusing God's invitation and abusing His messengers when they know full well what actions Herod or the Romans would take in such a situation.

That still doesn't mean that this is exactly how God views the situation. He is in the business of rescuing His people from His enemy. If His people insist on siding with that enemy they can't be rescued. Therefore Jesus uses a story of clear and present peril to life and limb to shake their complacency and hopefully allow a seed of doubt in their own self-righteousness to germinate.

And in the meantime, their refusal - in the story - gives the King reason to invite in everyone wandering the streets. Once again, this does not mean that the rest of us only get to access the Kingdom of God because those initially invited said "no" and murdered some prophets. God's plan all along has been to invite us all; the story is framed the way it is, in order to provoke the leaders of the Jewish nation to think about what they are doing.

But there is no mistaking the central point of both the core thread, and the "original invitees" thread: "this" is not complicated; you get an invitation, you turn up, you are in the wedding feast - and the Kingdom of God is just like that.

Okay, so what about the person with no wedding garment, and that problematic statement about many and few.

Let's start at the end, with that statement, "For many are invited, but few are chosen." In Greek that is πολλοὶ γάρ εἰσιν κλητοὶ ὀλίγοι δὲ ἐκλεκτοί (*polloi gar eisin klhtoi olio de eklektoi*).

It is true that ἐκλεκτοί (literally "called out" or "out-called") is normally used in a positive sense of picked out, selected, chosen etc. The problem is that in the context - where a huge crowd has been invited into the palace and a single improperly dressed person is thrown out - "many are called and few are chosen" simply doesn't fit.

Even if you factor in the invited guests from the start of the story, the best you could say would be "many are invited, but an even larger, and completely different, group of people are chosen".

So the first thing to notice is the (rather weak) pun. Even without Greek you can see it - κλητοὶ and ἐκλεκτοί are cognate words, and if you look long enough you will spot the κλ-τ (kl-t) pattern of consonants in both.

To retain this relationship, I would render this as "many are called, and a few are called out". That is still a perfectly accurate rendering, but it no longer assumes that ἐκλεκτοί is positive in this context.

We use the phrase "called out" in the sense of picking up on someone who has done wrong, and that is what we are seeing here as well; "called out" in a negative sense.[1]

The message then becomes clear, and it is exactly the same as the Parable of the Sower: there is this great invitation or opportunity (to be fruitful, to be part of the wedding feast) so don't let something stupid (hard heart, shallowness, cares and concerns or, in this case, lack of appropriate clothing) rob you of that.

So finally, what does it mean to not have a wedding garment on? Honestly, I am less clear on this, but I suspect it is the obvious. The obvious, to me, would be "you have been invited to a wedding feast at the King's palace; and you didn't make any effort to put on clothing that shows that you are sensible of the honour you have received? Are you disrespecting the King and His household?" Or, to put it more simply, there is a response expected, beyond just turning up.

At the very least, turn up clothed with wonder and amazement and joy and love and gratitude. Maybe a garment of praise would be appropriate.

What does this mean?

Once again, this Parable is really making a point that is the opposite of what we thought we were seeing here. The Kingdom of God is an open invitation - maybe even a very pressing one.

Is that important? My reading of things is that you and I have an enemy who wants us to believe that God is mad at people, mad

---

[1] The phrase πολλοὶ γάρ εἰσιν κλητοὶ ὀλίγοι δὲ ἐκλεκτοί also appears in Matt 20:16, but only in Textus Receptus. If you are unfamiliar with this term, it broadly means the Greek text Erasmus worked with in the early 16th Century, and which is based on the textual variations preferred and preserved by the Eastern (Orthodox) Church. My view is that Textus Receptus shows the same tendency towards religious massaging as do so many of our English translations. Now if πολλοὶ γάρ εἰσιν κλητοὶ ὀλίγοι δὲ ἐκλεκτοί is original to Matt 20:16 then it would rather undermine my point here; but a) the best texts omit this phrase and b) it doesn't logically fit there because that passage is about the first (or closest) being last (or furthest), and not at all about 'called' versus 'chosen' nor about missing out.

at us, willing to save only the few and not the many, and mostly interested in sending us to be persecuted and die for the Gospel.

That enemy will stop at nothing to pervert our view of God. He has been at it since the Garden when he managed to trick Adam and Eve into removing the crowns God had anointed them with and, by committing treason, hand over the Earth to him. This is the narrative of Scripture; why else does Jesus submit to being tested by Satan, or refer to him as "the prince of this world" in both John 14:30 and 16:11?

God is on a rescue mission. The one obstacle He faces is - ironically - us. You and I still have the authority He gave us from the beginning; and this means, that as long as we believe propositions which are not true - for example, that only few can ever be saved - then there is a good chance that we will speak with authority in such a way as to prevent God from being able to work.

You may well say, "but 'The Lord's hand is not shortened, that it cannot save.'" I mean, who can thwart God? The issue is when we fail to understand that He gave us authority on earth; and that He takes delegated authority far more seriously than we apparently do.

We forever think that we are waiting for God to act; but mostly He is waiting for us to speak, using our authority to align ourselves with what His word already says.

If that is so, then it is critically important that we see and agree with God's intention to save all, if possible. Otherwise you may find yourself working against God.

"For God so loved the world, that He gave His only Son, that **whoever** believes in Him might not be destroyed but have everlasting life." (John 3:16). "The harvest is **plentiful**, the labourers few - demand that the Lord of the Harvest drives out labourers into His harvest field." (Luke 10:2)

The picture between Mark 4 (the Sower) and Matthew 22 (the Wedding Feast) is consistent with these passages from Luke and John - once you hang the picture straight!

What does this mean for me?

This is still early in our journey together, but at least by the time you come back to read these chapters again, I would hope we might be in agreement that our response should be something more along the line of "my goodness, I need to be tooling up to handle the fantastic response rate when we actually start telling people Good News!"

Perhaps we should reference another feature of the Parable. The servants brought in the both the good and the bad from the street, and the King was apparently happy to see them there.

In passing, please note that the pairing of words used here as "bad as well as good", and elsewhere as "evil" and "good", πονηρος and ἀγαθος, actually mean "wretched / oppressed" and "noble / fit for purpose".

From the story, as far as we know, the King did not ask his servants to explain to his new guests that they were wretched oiks. For this, and other reasons, it is useful to question what we were taught (or what I was, at any rate); is it necessary to commence the Good News by telling people they are dreadful sinners and that God is mad at them? You will probably find that a good number **already** assume they are dreadful sinners; which should lead us to the question, "who told them that?"

If you were thinking I was making a cheap shot about 'Christians' or 'Christian TV', that isn't the answer I would give at all - ultimately, there is an accuser, and he isn't anything to do with God.

As a friend of mine pointed out recently, God actually asked Adam: "who told you that you were naked?" In other words, eating of the

Tree of the Knowledge of Good and Evil gives you the rational capacity to understand you might be deficient; but **it was someone you were talking to** who told you that you **were** deficient; the Accuser, who has his own agenda to get you down and hold you under.

Don't think for a moment I am questioning whether sin is real or really such a problem. I think the issue is that we think that sin is about what we do. Sin is actually who we are, as the family lineage of Adam and Eve, who through one act of treason, handed all their rule on earth over to God's worst enemy.

But now there is an answer, which sets you free and gives you a new identity as God's child and a member of His household.

If you are rescuing someone who has fallen into a septic tank, you don't have to get him to acknowledge that he is filthy before you pull him out. He kind of knows that already. But telling him you have a hose, a hot shower and a fresh change of clothes for him - that's good news.

So practically that might mean you want to rethink what Good News is, and what we are doing in extending the free gift of life to others. If it is true that eternal life is the free gift of God, then our job is not to search hearts, or fob people off with soft untruths; our job is to tell people that God isn't mad at them, that He loves them, and that if they call on the name of the Lord they have the right to become a child of God, with full access to His whole estate.

Good News, eh?

So, where to next?

I have referenced, somewhat in passing, the notion of **our authority** in this present chapter, and I wouldn't expect that to be easy to take on board (or maybe, once again I am just revealing what I myself found hard going!). So, next up, we are going on a boat voyage to learn more about what God expects of us in the Kingdom. A spot of gentle sailing across the Lake with Jesus would be just the ticket...

Chapter Three: All at Sea

Then he got into the boat and his disciples followed him. Suddenly a furious storm came up on the lake, so that the waves swept over the boat. But Jesus was sleeping.

The disciples went and woke him, saying, "Lord, save us! We're going to drown!"

He replied, "You of little faith, why are you so afraid?" Then he got up and rebuked the winds and the waves, and it was completely calm.

The men were amazed and asked, "What kind of man is this? Even the winds and the waves obey him!"

Matthew 8:23-27, NIV

What are we looking at here?

This passage appears to me to be one of the most-referenced episodes in Jesus' life and ministry. How it is referenced, is remarkably consistent: generally something to the effect that "life is full of troubles, but with Jesus in my boat, I can smile at the storm. We just need to wake Him up with our fervent cries for help when things get tough."

I am sure you have heard - or even given - that sermon, at least once a year. Last time I edited this chapter, I happened to go on LinkedIn afterwards and - what do you know, there was a picture of Jesus asleep in the boat and the disciples looking worried! We can't escape this narrative...

What's wrong with this picture?

This point of view is so common amongst Christians, and across all denominations, that it probably qualifies as universal Christian doctrine. Unfortunately, that doesn't mean it is correct. In fact, this passage should be conveying to us exactly the opposite message to the one we seem to have been hearing.

This won't be the last time I say this, but it seems to me that many of us spend our lives wondering, "when is God going to do something?" I certainly spent a lot of my life just like that, until someone set me straight.

Actually, God has already done everything, and given you everything, you need (read 2 Peter 1:3-4, John 19:28-30, for example). So if anything, He is asking - and with a great deal more justification - "when are **you** - My people - going to do something?"

What should we be seeing instead?

We really need to push the 'reset' button, if we are ever to understand this passage at all.

Here's the unvarnished story, just as it reads in the Greek:

And he got into the boat, his disciples following him. And behold, a great shock (or shaking) came upon the sea, so that the boat was covered by the waves - but he was sleeping. And going to him, they got him up, saying "Lord, save us, we are being destroyed."

And he said to them, "What cowards are you, little-faiths?" Then he got up, rebuked (literally, 'imposed a penalty on') the winds and the sea, and there came a great calm.

The men were amazed, saying, "what country is this man from, that even the winds and the sea submit to him?"

Matthew 8:23-27, my translation

So to summarise the differences from the version you have probably been reading:

+ **It wasn't a storm, furious or otherwise.** Matthew uses the Greek word σεισμὸς ('seismos'). Seismos literally means an earthquake, or more generally a shock or shocks (i.e. a shaking).

The picture painted is more like a hammer of wind slamming into the lake without warning, rather than a bit of dirty weather brewing up. It's a shock, in every sense of the word. Maybe a squall fits; but I have had a steel-frame tent destroyed by a sudden 'bolt' of wind during bush-fires in the Blue Mountains in Australia.

It could even have been an actual earthquake (the Sea of Galilee sits in a slow-shifting rift valley, after all), although the record is silent about any damage on land. Whatever it was, it was outside the experience of even those disciples who had previously made their living on the Sea.

+ **No one said "we are going to drown".** You can read the Greek word ἀπολλύμεθα ('apollumetha') as middle voice ('we are perishing') or as passive voice ('we are being destroyed'); I favour the latter from the context, in which case the implication is that the disciples knew they were under attack. Which leads to two further thoughts, which I will share in the next section.

+ **Jesus calls them little-faiths and asks them why they were such cowards.** There is no way around this: that is what δειλοί ('deiloi') means: cowards.

In Revelation 21:8, being δειλοῖς is a qualification for being thrown into the burning lake of fiery sulphur. We are used to the disciples being ὀλιγόπιστοι ('oligopistoi', little-faiths) but 'cowards' seems a bit harsh in the circumstances.

Jesus is being very specific, and if you understand why He says this, you will understand the whole passage correctly.

Now, the translators haven't helped, and the error appears to go back to all the most influential Reformation translators. Jerome got it pretty right in the Vulgate, translating δειλοί with the Latin *timidi*, which does mean 'cowards' as well as - unfortunately - shy or fearful. But Luther, Wycliffe and Tyndale all took a softer line and avoided the notion of "cowards", instead saying 'agaste' (Wycliffe), 'fearful' (Tyndale) or 'furchtsam' (Luther). Each generation since has softened it further.

⁕ **At the risk of splitting hairs, "what kind of man is this" is just too far from the original.** Ποταπός ἐστιν οὗτος ('potapos estin houtos') literally means 'from what country is this one', this one meaning Jesus - and if we stick with this literal interpretation, we will get the key to the underlying principle. (Ποταπός is a late spelling of ποδαπός, in case you are trying to look it up.)

What does this mean?

However you read the "shock" (as storm or earthquake or just the sea going nuts around them) it was out of the ordinary, and the disciples saw it as an attempt to destroy them, which is why they grabbed Jesus, pulled Him upright and shouted "Lord! Save! We are being destroyed!" at him.

So first up, full credit to them for not just saying "oh well, guess this is the end, so long..." They recognised they were under attack, and knew Jesus could turn back the attack.

What may not have been so helpful is their unwitting affirmation of disaster.

I have learnt (the hard way) that affirming that some bad thing is happening, gives it authority. What do I mean by that? They were shouting "we are being destroyed!"

If your response to bad news from your doctor or your accountant is to say "I am dying of cancer" or "I'm going bankrupt", what effect will that have on your situation? You may say, "it is just words". Well, words have power; but it is worse than that.

Out of the abundance of the heart, the mouth speaks. And your heart and mouth working together have authority. This is authority which you can use to agree with what God's Word says, OR with what your situation says. What you say is what is happening, and we have that on very good authority: yours.

So beware of digging a hole you are in, deeper with every sentence, as it forms in your heart and you find agreement with it.

We can get a kind of perverse pleasure out of saying just how bad things are. So this can be a **really hard habit** to break. But we need to beat it, if indeed we want to see the Kingdom in action. When you "get" this, you will understand why Satan almost never needs to do anything serious; a small hint of trouble and we start dooming ourselves with the words that flow out of what we believe in our hearts.

Maybe this is why Peter says that "Satan goes about **like** a roaring lion, seeking whom he may devour". He has no actual power, but instead is extraordinarily good at getting us to attack ourselves with the thoughts of our hearts and the words of our mouths.

So why does Jesus call them cowards?

Stop and ask yourself: **what is the one big difference between fear and cowardice?**

To understand, consider a battle front in the Second World War.

You are looking at a company's Main Line of Defence, a staggered string of fox holes, with outposts in front and company HQ behind. The enemy is advancing, firing their weapons. *How do you tell who is just fearful and who - if anyone - is cowardly?*

The first is easy. **Everyone is afraid.** I have listened to (or read in transcription) recordings of the oral histories of very many frontline soldiers of the twentieth century. Some of them have had the courage of lions; but I never yet heard one say he wasn't afraid. If you can see someone in a foxhole in the middle of a battle and they are still alive, they are afraid.

To pick out the cowards, you have to look a little harder. They are the ones crouched at the bottom of their foxhole, **not firing their weapon.** Or they may be **running away** to the back echelon, without any order to do so; but once again, how you tell that they are a coward is that they are **not doing what they should be doing** in the situation - resisting the enemy attack with their weapons.

Just to be clear - I am not making a moral judgement on anyone who lived through a combat situation here, I am just trying to nail the essential difference between fear and cowardice. Fear is an internal state. Cowardice is a failure to do your duty, a failure to do what you should be doing.

Jesus asked the disciples what kind of cowards they were. That suggests that He was telling them that **they had failed to do what they should have done.**

Which of course begs the question: what *should* they have done?

If the answer is in the story at all, then it can only be what happens next: Jesus speaks to the winds and the sea with the result that a great calm comes.

The phrase exactly mirrors the earlier phrase: first, a great shock comes; then a great calm comes. Presumably the one is as sudden (and shocking) as the other.

Jesus speaks to the winds and the sea: well, what does he say? In Matthew's version, we are not given the words, just the import of them, namely that he '*epitimao*'ed them.

ἐπιτιμάω (epitimao) is one of those interesting words which carries apparently opposite meanings. Originally it means to 'give worth to' - for example saying "you are a most excellent archer" - but it then takes on the sense of setting a penalty in the courts - for example telling someone the "worth" of their crime: "that little offence will cost you ten talents of silver". The meaning of rebuke then comes by extension, but at the very least it is a rebuke with teeth. "Do this, or else this is what it will cost you, and I am not kidding..."

Interestingly, Mark, in his account of this episode (Mark 4:35-41), tells us that Jesus' actual words were, "silence, you are (have been) muzzled" (Σιώπα, πεφίμωσο). That sure sounds like someone exercising authority by way of a rebuke.

Like the disciples, you may be thinking, "hold on, that is all very well, but this is **Jesus** speaking; I have no difficulty believing Jesus can tell creation to behave. But the disciples couldn't, and neither can I."

And that is our problem. We are labouring under a delusion. We think "Jesus was the Son of God, *so of course he could do all this stuff.*"

In order to hold this view, we have to suppress a lot of the Gospel narrative.

For example, we will need to file John 14:12 ("whoever believes in me will do the works I have been doing, and they will do even greater things than these") in the too-hard-to-understand basket. We also need to ignore every bit of training Jesus gave the disciples, the Sending Out of the Twelve, and of the Seventy-Two, and more.

So maybe it is time to go back and read all the Gospels with an open mind and heart, because we may have been missing something - actually, missing the whole point.

Yes, Jesus is most definitely the Son of God; but given that is so, why did he silence just about everyone who ever identified him by that title? Apart from Simon Peter, that one time, and His Heavenly Father's voice from heaven on a couple of occasions, He rebukes anyone calling Him the Son of God. His preferred self-referencing name is always "the Son of Man".

Well, those He silenced were always evil spirits speaking through possessed people; which is interesting in itself (i.e. why were evil spirits, of all things, so keen to make sure everyone knew He was the Son of God?) But surely all the miracles were done to demonstrate that he really was the Son of God?

Actually, Jesus made it clear that no amount of signs and wonders would be enough for an unbelieving generation - not even someone rising from the dead would convince them (see the parable of the Rich Man and Lazarus in Luke 16). Jesus was, and is, the Son of God, most definitely; but something else is going on here.

Now, you might say, "Jesus is the Son of God but preferred calling himself by the Messianic title, 'the Son of Man', that's all."

Which would be an extremely good point, except that nowhere in any biblical or rabbinical text is the term "Son of Man" by itself used with any Messianic reference. It is not a Messianic title, at all. It means Man, perhaps with extra emphasis; "you don't just *appear* to be a Man but you are a Son of Man - a man from a long line of men." **So what if Jesus was simply emphasising that he is operating as a Man?**

Replay the scene:

"What country is this man from?" asked the disciples. We think we know the answer - Jesus can do this because he is God's Son. But Jesus has asked the disciples why they are cowards, suggesting that they could - *and should* - have done what He then proceeds to do.

We are thinking Jesus is proving his divinity, but He is actually doing something of much more relevance to us.

He is modelling for us what **normal** looks like.

For a given value of normal, of course. Man separated from God and living in submission to a system imposed by man's worst enemy is not even remotely normal in Jesus' frame of reference.

Before the fall recorded in Genesis 3, Man had the authority on earth. Hebrews 2:6-8, which is quoting Psalm 8 and which is about Man (not Jesus) spells this out. So Jesus calls himself the Son of Man because he is the first normal Man on earth in a very long time - but he is definitely not the last.

To be normal, a man or woman has first to come home to the Kingdom of the Heavens - the Kingdom of God - which is where he or she belongs. That is why Jesus invests the vast majority of the time he has with his disciples explaining to them what the Kingdom of God is like: they need to be taken out of the cursed, fallen thinking that goes with the kingdom of this world, and renew their minds with the thinking that goes with their citizenship of the Kingdom of Heaven.

The words of Jesus in our Matthew 8 passage, only make sense if He was telling the disciples, "this is what you should have done: you tell it to STOP!"

So, in answer to the question, "what country is this man from, that even the winds and the sea pay heed to, submit to and obey him?", we need to answer, "ah, that would be the Kingdom of the Heavens, where every citizen is meant to exercise that kind of authority."

What does this mean for me?

If you didn't already have an inkling that this was true, you may be in shock (or some form of denial) right now. You might be saying, "but nothing in my life so far lines up with this!"

Okay, but believe me when I tell you that this is **very good news**. You were never designed to endure terrible things, waiting endlessly for the heavenly cavalry to come over the hill. Nor were you designed to have to look at yet another loss - a loved one dead before their life is fulfilled, a business failure, a financial loss or whatever - and say "oh well, God knows what's best."

Of course God knows best, *which is why* when you became His child and a citizen of His Kingdom, He gave you everything you needed for life and Godliness, through your knowledge of Him, the one who called you, and with access to all His great and precious promises (yes, I am just quoting 2 Peter 1:3-4 again).

But it doesn't matter how much God has given you or me, if when we face apparent disaster we just say, "God knows what He is doing. God is teaching me something by making me go through this. God will help me bear even this. It was this person's time to die..."

That attitude hammers the nails home in your own coffin - and tells a completely false story about your Heavenly Father who loves you so much that He gave Jesus, precisely so you wouldn't have to keep suffering loss in these situations. Really.

It might help if you pray this with me: *"Father God, I believe that you love me, and could not love me more. You are not mad at me, and you have given me all things. Help me Holy Spirit to understand the amazing inheritance that is mine, right now, in Christ Jesus, and show me how to walk in courage to claim victory in every single situation which confronts me. In Jesus Name, Amen"*

And if you are currently facing a terrible situation of some kind, face it and tell it to STOP. You do most certainly have the authority.

Yes, but...

This sounds a great idea when everything is going well. But if you are currently in some kind of crisis, and "on the back foot", then the last thing you feel like is someone who can tell anything to stop.

And here are the likely problems:

+ You **don't feel** like you have authority;

+ You do secretly think that it is your fault, somehow, and that therefore God **won't accept** you;

+ And you **can't think** of a helpful Word from scripture, to save your life.

In no particular order:

+ Whatever you are up against, the one thing you can be sure of is that it isn't God's fault, nor did God set up the situation to teach you a lesson.

  Is it your fault? It could be. Or not. Who cares? God isn't mad at you, He loves and accepts you, and is for you, and not against you. He had that signed, sealed and delivered long before whatever stupid things you (or I) may have done along the way. Go back and read Chapter Two again. If you haven't yet turned up at the party He invited you to, then that is definitely the place to start.

• You don't feel [insert anything in here]. Again, who cares? Really. In a court of law, do you think the judge rules based on what the accused feels? "You stole this family's life savings... and their cat!" "I don't *feel* guilty, your honour..." "Case dismissed!" No, in a court of law it is about facts and laws.

You have authority, whether you feel like it or not. The disciples had all the authority they needed to stop the storm, they just let their feelings overmaster them.

• Can't think of the right Scripture? Just stop a minute, because trying to pull Scripture out of the air isn't going to help you. What has God said to you? What promise has He made you, that you have been focusing on, internalising, meditating on? If the answer is really "nothing", then that is your problem right there.

Ask God to give you a Word you can stand on, and be good soil when it arrives. Don't let the seed bounce; it is your answer! (And the answer for a whole lot of other people, once you have brought it to harvest time. Re-read Chapter One if you need to.)

So, where to next?

I haven't tried counting this for myself (because I can think of a whole number of ways of defining the problem) but my impression is that what people say is true: Jesus did indeed speak more about **money** than He did about [insert your preferred comparison topic here]. So perhaps we should go there next.

Chapter Four: Hard to Follow

Just then a man came up to Jesus and asked, "Teacher, what good thing must I do to get eternal life?"

"Why do you ask me about what is good?" Jesus replied. "There is only One who is good. If you want to enter life, keep the commandments."

"Which ones?" he inquired.

Jesus replied, "'You shall not murder, you shall not commit adultery, you shall not steal, you shall not give false testimony, honor your father and mother,' and 'love your neighbor as yourself.'"

"All these I have kept," the young man said. "What do I still lack?"

Jesus answered, "If you want to be perfect, go, sell your possessions and give to the poor, and you will have treasure in heaven. Then come, follow me."

When the young man heard this, he went away sad, because he had great wealth.

Matthew 19:16-22, NIV

What are we looking at here?

The passage is pretty clear. Here is someone who receives exactly the same invitation as Simon and James and John and the others, to come and follow Jesus; and yet he can't do it, because his great wealth gets in the way.

This passage is fundamental to our understanding of how Jesus views money; not necessarily as bad in itself, but in excess, a huge hindrance to people being able to respond to the Gospel.

What's wrong with this picture?

Once again we need to be sure that we aren't reading that last sentence - "he went away sad, because he had great wealth" - as a complete summation of what just happened. In the parable of the wedding party in Chapter Two, we saw that what we might have thought was a summary actually contradicted what went before in the parable.

This time the account is of a real-life incident, but we should treat it with the same degree of care. The truth is, there are some unusual aspects to this interaction, which I can summarise as a list of questions:

- Why does Jesus tell the young man to keep the commandments?
- Why this particular (and peculiar) list of commandments?
- What does Jesus tell him to sell, and why?
- How much is he to give away?
- What is treasure in heaven?
- Is the young man gone for good?

The first of those questions should appear strange to anyone brought up with a 'Pauline' view of salvation; the others only take on their puzzling nature when we look carefully at the text.

What should we be seeing instead?

All three synoptic Gospels give us this story of the rich young man (Luke calls him a ruler) who went away from Jesus, sorrowful (actually more like 'vexed'), because of Jesus' advice to him. In each case this is followed by a passage in which Jesus uses a camel to explain that the Kingdom of God is very hard (impossible?) for rich people to enter.

You can find the story in Matthew 19:16-29, Mark 10:17-30 and Luke 18:18-30. We will follow Matthew's account as above, and we will save the camel (and what Jesus told the young man to sell) for our next chapter.

So, the young man comes to Jesus, addresses Him as "Teacher" and asks what "good deed" He must do in order to inherit eternal life (Luke and Mark have "Good Teacher" and just have him asking "what must I do"). After challenging him about his use of "good" - something which relates only to God - Jesus tells him that if he wants to enter life, he should keep the commandments.

"Which commandments?", the young man asks.

Jesus then quotes from the "other people" section of the Ten Commandments (if you know what I mean - the first four commandments deal with our behaviour towards God, the last six our behaviour towards other people).

What do you notice about the list Jesus quotes?

Yes it is out of order (compared to Exodus 20 and Deuteronomy 5), but what else?

That's right. He only quotes five of the six "other people" Commandments!

Lest we notice, He fills the gaps: in Matthew, He also adds in the 'other people' half of the "summary of the Law", i.e. "love your neighbour as yourself", which then makes six in total; in Mark there is also added "don't defraud", which is not part of the Ten; Luke just gives us the five that are actual Commandments.

But in all three synoptics, one of the last six of the Ten

Commandments is missing. This one:

You shall not covet your neighbour's house.
You shall not covet your neighbour's wife,
or his male or female servant,
his ox or donkey,
or anything that belongs to your neighbour.
(Exodus 20:17, NIV)

Which is interesting. After Jesus gives His (altered) list of Commandments, the young man is able to say, "all of these I have observed".

Is it significant that Jesus has let this rich young man off the hook, so that he **doesn't** have to testify about his adherence or otherwise to the Tenth Commandment, the one about coveting?

I suspect so. Of course, this was ultimately between Jesus and the young man, and none of our business; but the Tenth Commandment is mostly about money and wealth, which should only add weight to our perception that Jesus knew wealth was the big issue for this young man. Of course, it could have been that 'coveting his neighbour's wife' that was his problem; we just don't know.

But let us step back to the first question I raised: why on earth does Jesus tell the young man that "if you would enter life, keep the Commandments". Does Jesus really mean this, and if so is He contradicting what Paul writes later on, to the effect that no one can be justified under the Mosaic Law?

I don't think so. There is a different dynamic going on here.

The young man approaches Him (Mark says he ran up to Jesus) and addresses him as *didaskale* ("Διδάσκαλε", or teacher, which is, of course, equivalent to the Aramaic *"Rabbi"*). He asks Jesus what deed he can do to inherit eternal life. Jesus answers him with a stock Rabbinic answer: "if you want to enter into life, keep the commandments". Why does He do that?

Part of it is probably that "if you are going to call me Rabbi and ask me a Rabbinic question, you will get a Rabbinic answer." But that isn't the whole reason.

I think Jesus only does that, and then lists five commandments which He knows the young man **doesn't** have a particular problem with, in order to underline this fact: "you are doing pretty well as far as **this system** goes; and yet you know perfectly well **you don't have** eternal life. You know in your heart that you are still looking for something - and that is the real reason you have come to me. It isn't a good deed you need, you need Me."

So why did Jesus omit the Tenth Commandment from the list? Simply that if Jesus knew that the young man struggled to obey this one, He also knew that trying harder to obey this commandment was never going to set him free or give him eternal life. 'Commandment keeping' was not the real issue here.

Now you may argue that this is a subjective reading of the text on my part; and you are, of course, free to explain it as you choose. What happens next is less open to interpretation.

Jesus tells the young man that if he wishes to be complete (Matthew), or because he still lacks one thing (Mark and Luke), he should go, sell all he has, give (Matthew and Mark) or distribute (Luke) to beggars, have a treasury in heaven and "come, follow" Jesus.

Seems simple enough, but let's check what we are seeing here.

Jesus definitely tells the young man to sell everything he has. (We will come back to this in the next chapter). He tells him to give or distribute to beggars, but He does **not** lock this down as "give everything - all the proceeds of that sale to beggars". He strongly implies that this course of action will give him access to a treasury in the heavens. And He instructs him, "hither, follow me".

That is four actions: sell, give, have, follow. Working backwards through that list of four instructions, the first thing to note is that this rich young man (as we discover him to be by the end of the passage) is being instructed to **submit himself to Jesus' direction** from here on.

The phrase δεῦρο ἀκολούθει μοι ("hither, follow me") uses a formulation most often used with subordinate soldiers or slaves. It is definitely not "why don't we go along together, like two friends." It is far more peremptory than that and used between a master and a servant of some kind.

So this man of great means has to become like a subject, or even a slave, in order to accompany Jesus. That is no small thing. Money is power, influence, authority; Jesus makes it clear that the real answer for the young man lies in giving up his habitual sense of being in control, and in following Jesus like a servant.

Secondly, what is the **treasury in the heavens** the young man is to have? All three Gospel versions agree on this, except that Mark has "heaven" singular. So is this, literally, the famous "pie in the sky when you die?" Treasure in heaven, for later?

A treasury is - surprise - where you keep treasure. (Technically the Greek word θησαυρὸν can be used to mean either the treasure or the place you keep it, probably because, logically, a storehouse full of treasure is, itself - a treasure!) A treasury stores your resources, protects them from theft while keeping them available for use, when needed. The big question is **when** are you going to have needs, requiring the disbursement of treasure or money?

Will that be now, in this life; or in heaven, in your eternal life?

It seems kind of hard to picture a situation in God's presence, in God's house, where you might find yourself slapping your pockets and saying, "oh no, I left my wallet in my other golden robe".

No, resource is for **this** life: there are definitely no needs or lack in the Father's house when we get there. So a treasury - a strongroom - in the heavens, is a store of resource **for now**, that is kept safe in the heavens, where the enemy can't get to it - but you can.

I fear that for generations we may have been reading this the wrong way. A treasury in the heavens isn't money and resource stored up for a time when **money will be useless** and the available resource endless (that would be so cruel!). Θησαυρὸν ἐν οὐρανοῖς (a treasury in the heavens) is **for now**.

If we look quickly at the parallel passage in Luke 12, where Jesus makes this same offer and promise to His existing disciples (Luke 12:33), He says ποιήσατε ἑαυτοῖς βαλλάντια μὴ παλαιούμενα, θησαυρὸν ἀνέκλειπτον ἐν τοῖς οὐρανοῖς

"Make for yourselves purses that don't perish, an uninterruptible [or incessant, or infinite] treasure house in the heavens"

I don't know about you, but an uninterruptible treasure house (let alone an infinite one) sounds to me like a really useful asset to have, when you have an assignment to get done on earth.

So what was Jesus saying to the young man? Something like, "think you are rich now? You are not going to be the loser here, if you heed My instruction."

So, thirdly, **how much** was Jesus asking the young man to give to beggars? (We will talk about the meaning of πτωχοῖς elsewhere, but it isn't just the working poor; it is literally "one who cringes" and designates beggars, not those with little.)

In the light of what we just said, **does it actually matter?** If following Jesus' instructions was going to give you full-time access to an unbreakable bank, would you be trying to work the percentages on what you already have?

If you are worrying about how much you need to hold back, you probably haven't understood what is on offer here, yet!

On the other hand, in that parallel passage in Luke 12, addressed directly to His existing disciples, Jesus specifies that they are to liquidate their assets, and to **give alms** (*Luke 12:33*), or in the Hebrew term, *tzedakah* (צדקה), to beggars. In other words, turn your assets to cash, and do what is right in the culture by giving a portion - often a tenth - of the proceeds to those in need.

Is this what Jesus is saying to the young man - liquidate your assets and give alms - a tenth - from that? The truth is, we don't know! I think you could argue either case - 10% or 100% - equally convincingly. But on balance, the process is probably significant: sell all you have and give to the poor contains an unnecessary step if you are going to give *all* of the proceeds to the poor; why not just say "give everything you have to beggars"? Why go to the trouble of selling it all?

"But," you may say, "surely the fact that the young man went away filled with sorrow, demonstrates that he knew Jesus was asking for the whole lot?"

Not necessarily. Let us assume that **whatever** it was the young man was hearing, it was something so momentous that it would take him time (and sorrowful consideration) to work out. And "follow me like a nobody" could well have been the hardest part. That still fits with the final statement about his great wealth; he is wealthy and therefore powerful and yet Jesus invites him to follow Him like a servant or slave.

But that does bring us to the crux of the young man's story. What was the point in Jesus telling him to sell everything he had? We'll get to this in the next chapter.

What does this mean?

I hope we might have injected at least an element of uncertainty into your previous reading of this passage. Whatever it is, this story is not as simple as just "Rich man can't face loss of everything, turns back."

From the structure of the passage and Jesus' interaction with the young man, it is clear that the most important element is not the money, but the culmination to which Jesus' instruction of the young man is leading - "hither, follow me".

Secondly, Jesus does not promise the young man pie in the sky but rather a treasury for now, which must mean provision and almost certainly the availability of money.

So what Jesus was asking the young man to do, would - primarily - set him free to follow Jesus; and secondarily, it would give him access to provision. As we said earlier, this suggests that whether he was to give away 100% or 10%, or something in between, wasn't actually a big deal (though some 'alms-sized' quantum seems most likely to me). The primary issue was "will you get free in order to follow me?"

This was also the issue for Peter and Andrew, James and John, when Jesus called them to follow Him. James and John left their business with their father Zebedee and the hired men; we are less sure what happened to Peter and Andrew's boat and nets, but we know Peter at least was married and had a mother-in-law as well as a wife, both of whom needed to be provided for; in neither case is it recorded that they had to shut down or sell their business; they all just left them behind and followed. Peter at least still had a boat in which to go fishing, in the final chapter of John's Gospel.

So again, I suggest, it is 'the following' that matters, the most.

What does this mean for me?

Well, how about this: there isn't a **system of behaviour** you can stick to that will give you eternal life, and actually you know it. If you have been thinking that to really follow Jesus you would have to **give up** everything, which you don't have the freedom to do at the moment: that probably isn't the biggest issue. Can you **follow** Jesus right now, and if not, what is holding you back?

And, definitely just between you and Him, **if** He was going to play the "keep the commandments / which ones?" game with you right now, which one(s) would He need to leave out in order to spare your embarrassment. Because that could be part of the answer to the "what is holding you back" question, too.

Just remember this: He isn't mad at you, and He wasn't mad at the young man, either. He is inviting you to follow Him, **for your own sake**, and into a position where all your needs will be met, in a very concrete and entirely non-mystical-distant-future manner.

So, where to next?

We're not finished with the young man, nor with Money and the Rich, yet. Time to thread a Camel through a Needle.

Chapter Five: Threading Camels

Then Jesus said to his disciples, "Truly I tell you, it is hard for someone who is rich to enter the kingdom of heaven. Again I tell you, it is easier for a camel to go through the eye of a needle than for someone who is rich to enter the kingdom of God."

When the disciples heard this, they were greatly astonished and asked, "Who then can be saved?"

Jesus looked at them and said, "With man this is impossible, but with God all things are possible."

Matthew 19:23-26, NIV

What are we looking at here?

Even more than the preceding verses, which we examined in the last chapter, this passage makes it clear that the Kingdom of Heaven is not for those with money. Jesus uses a comparison in which a clearly impossible thing is said to be more easily done than getting a rich person into the Kingdom of God. The only spark of hope for the wealthy comes where Jesus says that "impossible for man" doesn't mean "impossible for God".

What's wrong with this picture?

So many feet have trampled over this particular piece of ground, explaining, mitigating, clarifying, and so on - but all without apparently noticing some pretty fundamental features of this short passage.

The starting point is to go back and rethink what exactly Jesus told the rich young man to do, because it definitely **isn't** just "give away everything you have, so that you become poor, because only poor people can enter the Kingdom of God". Not at all!

But once we have cleared that up, we still have some problems to deal with:

+ Jesus doesn't use the word "hard" to describe rich people trying to enter the Kingdom of Heaven.

+ Using the word "hard" also spoils the really excellent joke He is making;

+ but then the disciples didn't get the joke either;

+ They - the disciples - weren't astonished, they were terrified,

+ and then... well, perhaps we should just work our way through what the story really says!

What should we be seeing instead?

We need to back up, a little, to our rich young man and the instruction Jesus gave him.

"Sell what you possess" (*Matt 19:21, NIV. Mark has "Sell what you have" and Luke, "Sell all you have"*)

What is the implication for the young man of this instruction? Is Jesus telling all of His disciples that they should have nothing? Or is there something else at work here?

To answer this, we need to consider the nature of possessions. We live (most of us, anyway) in a consumerist society. If I say "your possessions" to you, you will picture a whole raft of things, from large items like your car, possibly a house, maybe a boat, all the way down to small ones like your hairdryer, your dumbbells and your wireless headphones. It is all the stuff you have (or more likely, all the stuff that has you).

First century Judea wasn't that kind of society. (Most societies in human history weren't). Working up from the bottom, you had beggars (who had nothing), day labourers (who had nothing as soon as the work dried up) and then people of property, who had something. What did that look like?

Perhaps in passing we should first note that a study of the Old Testament law ought to convince you that God's intention was always for the people of Israel to be people of property; the year of Jubilee, for example, was meant to correct for individual failures along the way and get a family back into their land and property.

God did not draw the Israelites out of Egypt by promising to take them to a land where they could be poor but free; He promised them a land flowing with milk and honey, houses to live in which they didn't build, orchards they didn't plant and so on. It was a promise of prosperity, where they would each own property.

But what did that "property" look like, in First Century Judea?

Well, property could be a house with a workshop in it, if you were, say, a potter or other artisan. Jesus probably grew up in such a setting. It could be a shop and warehouse, and maybe some camels or donkeys if you were a trader or merchant. It could be a farm, or a vineyard, with a barn or storehouses, and a big house or a little one. The pattern you should be spotting is that property was primarily oriented around having **the means of producing wealth**.

Secondly, we live in an age where your father may have been a banker but you decide to be a computer programmer or a jazz bassist. Or vice versa; maybe your dad plays jazz bass and you are the banker. When your dad dies, you may well inherit his old bass fiddle, but you probably won't know what to do with it. That was his bag, not yours.

In first century Judea, sons tended to follow in their father's footsteps. Joseph was a carpenter, so Jesus learnt that trade too; and the obvious corollary of that is that the means of production tended to be passed down from one generation to the next, as well. That might be just a loom or a potter's wheel or a set of chisels; or it might be extensive estates, with houses, warehouses, pastures, barns, crop land, grain stores, vineyards and cellars.

The further implication of this is that (except for the smallest 'one man and his son' artisanal operations), **you almost certainly had household servants**, stewards and labourers working for you.

So property wasn't primarily how many Apple devices or surfboards you owned; it often had **a lot of human responsibilities** tied up with it.

This is reflected in the word for possessions used by Matthew in 19:21, *huparchonta* ("ὑπάρχοντα"). Mark and Luke just say "what you have" or "all you have" but ὑπάρχοντα is not only used here in Matthew 19, but is also the word used in the Luke 12 passage mentioned briefly in the last chapter, and to which we shall return later. In total, the word appears 14 times in Luke, and 3 times in Matthew. Let us dig a little deeper in order to understand the significance of this.

The NIV translates ὑπάρχοντα as wealth or possessions, but that barely does it justice. The word actually means "to begin or take the initiative" and, by extension, "to **be** the beginning" or "to **already be** in existence."

It is that last meaning - "to already be in existence" which allows this word to be used as a placeholder for "wealth" or "possessions". What kind of wealth or possessions does ὑπάρχοντα point to? **Inherited wealth**; that is, what your family **already had**, and has had '**from the beginning**'. The best English translation I can suggest in most contexts is "your estate".

There are endless Greek words for things you own, household goods, land and so on. For example:

+ *ploutos* ("πλοῦτος") is wealth,

+ *periousios* ("περιούσιος") is stuff you possess,

+ *kthmata* ("κτήματα", plural) are chattels (this is the word used in Matthew 19:22 "for he had many chattels")

+ but *kthma* ("κτῆμα", singular) is often a piece of real, i.e. land-based, property,

+ *pragmata* ("πράγματα") is just stuff (things) and

+ *chrhmata* ("χρήματα") is goods, property but especially in the sense that we would say of someone, "he has made his **pile**."

Jesus also uses *huparchonta* in Luke 12:15 when He is warning the crowd about all kinds of covetousness. (See - He didn't just happen to forget the tenth commandment when He spoke to the rich young man.) The context of Luke 12:15 is the episode in which a man asks Jesus to get his brother to share the inheritance with him.

If Jesus wanted to warn the crowd against wealth itself, he would have said *ploutos* or possibly *chrhmata*. If he wanted to warn them against owning land, he might have said *kthma*; if simply against having possessions of various kinds, he might have used *periousios*, *kthmata* or *pragmata*. But instead he talks about *huparchonta* which in its essence is "an advantage that has come down to you". His exact words are:

Ὁρᾶτε καὶ φυλάσσεσθε ἀπὸ πάσης πλεονεξίας, ὅτι οὐκ ἐν τῷ περισσεύειν τινὶ ἡ ζωὴ αὐτοῦ ἐστιν ἐκ τῶν ὑπαρχόντων αὐτῷ.

See, and guard against, all taking advantage [of others], [or

arrogant greed] because the life of someone is not in the degree to
which he gets more out of the family estate [i.e. inherited wealth]

It is a hard sentence to render into English, but I think it is more specifically about inheritance than the NIV's "life does not consist in an abundance of possessions."

Step back a moment. Think about the possessions you own because you have worked hard, been paid and then bought the item or items. (If you happen to be one of David's mighty men, you might want to think about something you acquired by going out and smiting some Philistines. It is the same thing. You worked hard for it.)

Now think about something you have inherited, from a parent or grandparent. Any difference?

Well, of course, you worked for the one and just received the other. But there is another difference.

Stuff you earn is yours, by right. Stuff you inherit tends to come with strings attached: **obligations**, expectations.

For example, I have my late, Great Aunt Maudie's fish knives and forks. I couldn't have disposed of those fish knives and forks without also hoping that my mother never, ever found out. It would have been seen as letting the family down. *"How could you...?"*

Well, that's half a dozen fish knives. Perhaps for you it is a silver clothes brush or a box of medals or a family tapestry. What then if you had inherited a vineyard? Or a working farm? A business with 1000 employees?

Inherited wealth carries a lot of expectation; and expectation **ties you down**. And that is a key to understanding what Jesus is saying to the rich young man.

A young man of wealth and, in Luke's version at least, power, comes to Jesus, asking what to do in order to gain the eternal life he knows he currently lacks. After getting him to confront the fact that just keeping the commandments isn't his answer, Jesus instructs him to liquidate his estate, give alms (or, alternatively, give it all away) in return for a heavenly treasury, and follow Him.

In other words, he is to relinquish **his pre-existing commitments** to family, businesses, employees and servants. Why? Because he needs to be fully present and available in order to follow Jesus. He can't be splitting his time between listening to Jesus and trying to sort out a dispute between two of his stewards or fixing the price of oil for the current olive crop.

Does this mean that Jesus is telling His disciples they cannot engage in business? No, he is simply telling **this** would-be disciple that he needs to start over with a clean slate. Doesn't mean that he wouldn't at some time in the future find himself managing all kinds of financial resources and productive enterprises; just means that it wouldn't help him now. For now, anything he brings along with him if he follows Jesus will be **encumbrances**.

Of course there is always a question of where your trust is: God or money? Money and wealth is great, useful and necessary; but it is a lousy master. The young man needs a chance to learn that for himself. Absolutely: but I am not sure that that is what this passage is about. "Liquidate your encumbrances, give alms, leave the rest somewhere safe or with the bankers, but drop your load, soldier and follow Me, without distraction".

Unfortunately, this is all rather academic: when the young man heard what Jesus had to say, his face fell and he went away sorrowful and sad, because he had great possessions (*kthmata* in Matthew and Mark) or riches (*plousios* in Luke).

Now stop, right there. What happens next?

If you are reading in an English translation, you probably think the answer is that Jesus (as it were) shrugs, says "so you see, it is **really hard for a rich person to enter the Kingdom of God.**"

In other words, this young man has refused eternal life, and that is pretty much what you can expect from rich people.

Jesus then goes on to compare rich people entering the Kingdom of God to getting a camel through the eye of a needle, which is a rather weird metaphor and has led in turn to various efforts to make the saying seem less weird.

In the process we have had two main suggestions: a) that there was a gate in Jerusalem called the Eye of the Needle (for which there is **absolutely zero evidence**) and before which camels had to kneel - humble themselves - in order to get through; or b) that the word isn't *kamhlos* (camel) but *kamilos* (rope). I am convinced both are wrong.

In His camel metaphor, Jesus is being very precise and very funny.

So what actually does He say?

The wording varies slightly in the three versions, but what they all have in common is the word *duskolws* ("δυσκόλως"); and *duskolws* is the adverbial form of the adjective which means "hard to satisfy" or "peevish". It **never** means "difficult" (except possibly in the sense, "he is being difficult, i.e. peevish" That is a **different word** from 'difficult' in the sense of saying "it is difficult to do such and such a thing.")

Matthew's version reads: "Truly I say to you that the rich enter the Kingdom of the Heavens, **peevishly.**"

Mark and Luke both have: "how **peevishly** those having a pile of wealth enter into the Kingdom of God".

So the first thing to notice is that Jesus says, in effect, "this is *how* the rich enter the Kingdom", not "it is difficult for the rich to enter". He is saying that they come in, **making a big fuss**; He does **not** say that they cannot get in.

Bonus question: *is Jesus expecting the rich young ruler to be back, sometime? **Now** you can say, "quite probably, yes…"*

And secondly, He is setting the stage for His camel joke. If there is any creature under heaven more peevish than the camel, I would hate to meet it. (Oh, that's right: rich people entering the Kingdom of Heaven. Whoops.)

So Jesus goes on to say that it is easier to get a camel through a hole in a pin (i.e. through the eye of a needle), than a rich man into the Kingdom of God.

The word He uses for "easier" is very specific, too. *eukopwteron* ("εὐκοπώτερον") is the comparative of *eukopos* ("εὔκοπος"), which is literally the prefix for "good" plus a word meaning "striking, beating, hardship, suffering or toil". In other words, it is still hard work, but it is much better work than the alternative. (If you had a good workout at the gym this morning, where you pushed yourself hard but aced it, that was arguably εὔκοπος).

So here, on the one hand you have a camel (which we presume and hope is a one-humped dromedary rather than a two-humped Bactrian camel) and you need to thread it through the eye of a needle. Just imagine the peevish complaints you are going to get from the camel, and that's even before you get to the hump. Talk about a big fuss!

And over here, on the other hand, is a rich man who needs to get into the Kingdom of God.

You have a choice - which will you help?

Jesus says, choose the camel; **it is way less fuss, every time**.

I know that a joke explained is a joke deflated, but you really should be laughing out loud at this point. And what happens next is even funnier.

The disciples were scared senseless (*exeplhssonto* "ἐξεπλήσσοντο", an extremely strong expression of terror) and cried out "then who can be saved?"

From this we can deduce that **none of the disciples were without wealth** (they weren't saying, "well I'm okay, but I *am* a little worried about my wealthy auntie Deborah"; **no**! They are reacting as those who have **just lost the certainty** of their own salvation).

That, of course, isn't the funny part. The funny part is that they hadn't got the joke.

Have you ever made a really hilarious joke and had someone think you were being **deadly serious**? What do you do next? You look them in the face to see if the penny is going to drop.

Sometimes they do eventually get the joke, and laugh. Sometimes they don't, even with the visual prompt of you looking expectantly at them. At that point, you are usually trying to keep your own laughter under control.

Or as it says in both Matthew and Mark, "Jesus looked them in the face..."

Or in other words, "Really? You are not getting this, are you..."

So when Jesus says, "with men this is impossible, but with God everything is possible", you have to ask - given His track record on intentional misdirection for effect - whether the "this" He is talking to them about is a) the task of getting rich people into the Kingdom or b) the task of turning the disciples into men who can 'keep up' with the story they are in? And I do make this suggestion in all seriousness.

What does this mean?

As users of English translations of the New Testament, we have all been reading something which isn't actually there. Jesus **never said** it was hard for the rich to enter the Kingdom, just that they make a lot of fuss as they enter.

Secondly, there should be a bigger question in our minds now about why Jesus told the rich young man to sell all he had. Was it because he needed to have all that wealth stripped away, or was it because his estate had him too tied up in responsibilities and other people's expectations, to be able to follow Jesus freely.

And when he walked away sorrowfully, was he worrying about money or about what all his family and retainers were going to think if he sold up?

Lastly, if the notion that Jesus made jokes troubles you, don't worry about it. It is hard to imagine the disciples being **so** drawn to Jesus (a group of active men living and working together) and yet all spending every minute as solemn as owls; but that isn't the main thing here. Following Jesus is what we are about.

What does this mean for me?

It would be easy to encourage you to ask those obvious questions, about what is holding you back from following Jesus fully. But honestly, unless the Holy Spirit is putting His finger on something in your life and saying "deal with this so we can move forward", I am not sure you will get very far down that line.

Responding to Him is fruitful; endless introspection about what you might be doing wrong is not.

The harder assignment might be this: ditching well over a thousand years of accumulated deep untruth about the Kingdom of God in relation to property. The Kingdom is **not** a place to come and be "poor but contented" together. Our thinking needs to change. As I have said in the Prologue, good luck trying to accomplish your assignments for God without provision.

I hope that we can all agree now that Jesus didn't say it is hard for rich people to be saved.

Turning up for a party, remember? Rich people are good at that. Losing unhelpful encumbrances so as to follow Jesus - maybe we are all rich enough that we are going to make a fuss about that one...

So, where to next?

In order to secure this piece of ground that needs to be reclaimed, perhaps we should go back to the beginning, and the first record we have of Jesus' actual words spoken in a Synagogue, and try to understand what He read out and why.

Chapter Six: Very Good News

Jesus returned to Galilee in the power of the Spirit, and news about him spread through the whole countryside. He was teaching in their synagogues, and everyone praised him.

He went to Nazareth, where he had been brought up, and on the Sabbath day he went into the synagogue, as was his custom. He stood up to read, and the scroll of the prophet Isaiah was handed to him. Unrolling it, he found the place where it is written:

> *"The Spirit of the Lord is on me,*
> *because he has anointed me*
> *to proclaim good news to the poor.*
> *He has sent me to proclaim freedom for the prisoners*
> *and recovery of sight for the blind,*
> *to set the oppressed free,*
> *to proclaim the year of the Lord's favor."*

Then he rolled up the scroll, gave it back to the attendant and sat down. The eyes of everyone in the synagogue were fastened on him. He began by saying to them, "Today this scripture is fulfilled in your hearing."

All spoke well of him and were amazed at the gracious words that came from his lips. "Isn't this Joseph's son?" they asked.

Luke 4:14-22, NIV

What are we looking at here?

Jesus Himself asserted that this verse-and-a-bit from Isaiah 61:1-2 was crucial to understanding His ministry.

"Today **this scripture** is fulfilled in your hearing." All He had done was read the passage, and then made His short statement about fulfilment; so, the message must be, He Himself is the fulfilment of the one described in Isaiah 61.

What does this tell us about Jesus? The content of the passage He read is significant. Four of the statements have intended recipients, and there is a common thread: they are the poor, the prisoners, the blind, the oppressed. Jesus has come for those who are experiencing hardship, to bring them good news, freedom, recovery of sight, and setting free (which repeats the second item in the list). Only the fifth and final "blessing" - proclamation of the year of the Lord's favour - is without a specific 'audience'.

It is not unreasonable therefore to suggest that, based on this episode, the mission upon which Jesus has been sent has a set of clearly defined beneficiaries; and they are not those who are doing well out of life.

In the context of the previous chapters of this book, surely this passage pushes the balance back the other way; there is no way it can be stood on its head. Jesus was sent for those who have suffered in life, not those who have done well. The poor, prisoners, the blind, the oppressed; that's who He came for.

You may see a further significance in the passage Jesus read out: what He **didn't** read. Jesus ended His reading from Isaiah 61 with "to proclaim the year of the Lord's favour". But He has stopped halfway through a sentence; the rest of the sentence reads "...and the day of vengeance of our God!" Jesus' hearers in the Synagogue would have known this too; as has often been pointed out, it was as if an unspoken threat hung there like a noose. Better respond to Yahweh's favour, or you might suffer Elohim's vengeance.

What's wrong with this picture?

There are a couple of rather big assumptions implicit in the picture I have given above.

If I told you that I had a mission to help sick people, there are two ways you could understand me. I could be saying that I have set up an organisation to make sick people more comfortable while they suffer and/or die. Or you could assume I was running an organisation which **cured** sick people of their ailments. Both are possible. The first is palliative in its objectives; the second curative.

For reasons I simply don't understand, whenever Jesus talks about the poor, the Church seems to have mostly understood His mission as palliative. The only possible justification I can see is one comment Jesus makes, to the effect that "the poor you will have always." (Matthew 26:11, Mark 14:11 and John 12:8). In the context though, this does not seem a reasonable connection to make, i.e. that every pronouncement of Jesus about the poor is based on the assumption that they will always be poor. God clearly loves the poor and needy, but that doesn't mean He wants to keep them that way.

So let me ask two questions that might change your outlook, straight away. I say that because once asked, the first of these questions almost answers itself, and the second should (but probably doesn't):

+ If you were poor, what would be good news?

+ Upon whom, does God intend His vengeance to be wreaked?

What should we be seeing instead?

Let's start with an easy question: **did Jesus come to announce good news to the poor?**

The passage from Luke, above, certainly suggests that He did.

The Spirit of the Lord is on me,
because he has anointed me
to proclaim good news to the poor.

Let's look first at the exact meaning of a key word here.

The Greek word πτωχοῖς ("*ptwchois*") translated as "poor" in Luke 4:18 is more accurately rendered as "those who cringe" or "beggars". This Greek word πτωχοῖς is a good translation of the Hebrew of Isaiah, where *anawim* ("עֲנָוִים", again translated as "poor" in the NIV of Isaiah 61:1) comes from a root *anah* ("עָנָה") which has the same sense, of being physically pressed down, as "cringing" does, and is often translated "bowed down" or "afflicted".

So while this is definitely about poor people, the modern equivalent would be more like "homeless people", and definitely not just "the working class". Victor Hugo's term, *les misérables*, might capture the same thought; it is those who are **wretched**.[1]

So clearly, Jesus has come to announce good news to the wretchedly poor. As I asked earlier, **what would that good news for the poor look like?**

Before you answer that question, try this one. Based on what you know of Jesus' ministry, what would you say that **good news for the physically blind** would look like?

- Probably getting their sight back. Which is in fact what Isaiah 61:1 says (or rather the *Septuagint* Greek version of Isaiah 61:1 does, which Luke records Jesus as quoting).

What about **good news for the lame and paralysed**?

- Leaping up and walking around again, I guess.

Good news for the bereaved parent?

- Their son or daughter getting off the bier or the bed, and carrying on with their life.

---

[1] As an aside, Paul uses πτωχοί to explain the mission he is on in Romans 15:26, carrying "a contribution for the poor among the Lord's people in Jerusalem." This is apparently during the great famine of Claudius's time. It is therefore a description of "those who have been beggared [by the famine]"; not a suggestion that the Church in Jerusalem includes a number of beggars who are happy to live on handouts from believers elsewhere.

So what would **good news for the wretchedly poor** look like?

If you answered anything **other** than "getting out of poverty and enjoying prosperity", please stop and ask yourself, "why did I say that?" It might help to read through the whole of Isaiah 61. It is hard to avoid seeing how strong God's desire is to bless His people with financial and material prosperity - conspicuous prosperity that will make them stand out among the nations.

So proclaiming "good news to the poor" must include a way out of poverty. That isn't to say there is a magic wand that removes poverty from the earth, any more than God's covenant of healing just empties the hospitals. We always have our part to play; but good news for the poor must mean there is a way in which they can leave poverty behind them.

That is the first of my questions answered; what about the second one: the object of God's vengeance?

Consider that "noose left hanging in the air" by Jesus when He stopped reading halfway through Isaiah 61:2 (actually, whether Jesus would have seen verse divisions marked in the scroll is a somewhat vexed question; but He clearly stops part way through the Hebrew sentence).

Are we hearing the 'nice' part of Jesus' assignment, with the 'nasty' Day of Vengeance still to come?

As I suggested earlier, the primary question here is "**upon whom does God intend to wreak His vengeance?**"

Let's keep it simple. You wreak vengeance upon your enemy. So who is God's enemy?

"Fallen Man." "Unbelievers." "[Insert religious / philosophical /

ethnic community of choice here]." "Most people." "Me."

These five possible answers have in common, not only the fact that they are 100% wrong, but also that they betray what the problem is: if any of these seem a reasonable answer to you, you have most certainly been led astray by the Great Liar.

God's Day of Vengeance is wreaked upon SATAN.

The process of setting YOU, and billions like you, free from bondage - poverty, prison, blindness, illness and Satan's rule - is a big part of that vengeance. Let me say it again: we are not the OBJECTS of God's vengeance; if anything, we ARE His vengeance!

Let's read a more literal rendering of Isaiah 61:1-3 (the Hebrew version, this time):

The Spirit of Adonai Yahweh upon me
Because Yahweh has anointed me to bear good news to the wretched
He has sent me to bind up the brokenhearted heart
To proclaim to the captives release
And to the bound, the opening
To proclaim the year of Yahweh's favour
And the day of vengeance of Elohim to comfort all mourners
To console mourners in Zion
To give them beauty for ashes
The oil of joy for mourning
The garment of praise for the spirit of heaviness
That they may be called oaks of righteousness
The plantation of Yahweh
That He may be glorified

Isaiah 61:2-3, my rendering
based on Biblehub Interlinear Hebrew
(Westminster Leningrad Codex)

The day of vengeance of Elohim comforts all mourners.

So who mourns? Those who have suffered loss.

Why does any human being suffer loss? Ultimately because of the curse that Man himself imposed upon the earth when they (Adam and Eve) **were deceived by Satan**, who stripped them of their position and took their crowns for himself.

So comfort comes to mourners when they see **justice executed upon that Deceiver** - and **definitely not** when they see God's anger consume most of the people they know and love.

Secondly, in these three verses from Isaiah 61, which hinge around the day of vengeance, we see blessing for all God's people. Before the day of vengeance, it is all about good news, release and healing; after the day of vengeance it is all about restoring, rebuilding and replanting.

Now if you were a Jew, yes, you would read this passage in reference only to the Jewish people. It would therefore be possible (though by no means necessary) to imagine *all Israel's earthly enemies* as the objects of God's wrath.

But with the coming of Jesus, we understand the scope of God's promise of blessing. It is not just Israel but also 'people from every tribe and tongue and nation and people'. Because of that we can safely conclude that the day of vengeance is not aimed in the first instance at people at all; it is meant to comfort and restore people.

But we do have to confront a painful reality. Are we saying that *no people* will be caught up in "the Day of Vengeance" when it reaches its final act?

Well, from Satan's point of view, we are in the Day of Vengeance **right now**: it began when Jesus cried out "it is accomplished" on the cross, and it has been one long nightmare desperate retreat for him ever since. But yes, there is a time when that Day will reach its climax, and end. And yes, it is quite likely that men and women will be caught up in that destruction. All we can say is that if people refuse to break their allegiance to the kingdom of this world and its ruler, and so perish as a result, **that is not by God's will**, but rather by their own authority and choice - the authority God gave them from the beginning.

We can say this because the Father could not have done more to save the world of people. He made available a path to escape from that kingdom marked for destruction, and into the safety of the His own Kingdom and household and family. There comes a day when He says "enough"; and at that moment all options collapse to a single point; and books are opened.

But it is all still to play for (from our perspective in time); which is why Satan will do anything he can to get your thinking about this all twisted up.

As I said in the Prologue, Saddam Hussein never invented the concept of "human shields"; Satan has played that game since the Garden. *"If they are tied to me by their treason, God can't destroy me without destroying those whom He loves also."*

So to close the circle, why did Jesus stop reading Isaiah 61 at the point where He did? If you have followed the discussion above, then you know He wasn't giving a glimpse of 'the mail fist of judgement beneath the velvet glove of salvation', as so many appear to have thought. I would suggest instead that He was shielding His assignment from being seen and understood too soon.

And based on everything we have said above, it is very clear who Jesus wanted to keep in the dark about His and His Father's intentions: the object of that vengeance. Satan.

One major thread that runs through all of Jesus' instruction to His disciples, is "learning to keep your enemy in the dark". (I **didn't** say that it gets mentioned in church very often.)

Of course, Satan wants you to believe that he is on a par with God and knows the innermost thoughts of your mind. Nothing could be further from the truth.

If he sometimes seems to know what you are thinking, that is probably because you have faithfully germinated the seeds of fearful ideas he has been feeding to you. But he is a created being, gnawed by fear and uncertainty himself, and wholly reliant on human beings for all his intelligence (in the military sense, not the brain-power one).

We need to learn to be like Jesus. Speak only what you need to speak, to the right people and at the right time, and otherwise, keep your powder dry. Like Jesus, you are under no obligation to tell other people everything God has told you for your own understanding.

So with reference to the Isaiah passage, Jesus knew He was on a direct course for bringing about the Day of Vengeance, but He wasn't about to flag that to His enemy.

Satan at this point was still totally in the dark and hoping the agenda was something to do with 'displaying a bit of Godly power, through tricks with bread and healing and so on'. He was probably confident he could counter anything on that front.

As Paul said later, "None of the rulers of this age understood it [God's plan], for if they had, they would not have crucified the Lord of glory." (1 Corinthians 2:8) Jesus was the last person who was going to give the game away by what He said.

What does this mean?

There are two messages we have covered in this chapter.

Firstly, 'good news for the poor' is not some kind of message of solidarity from a socialist Kingdom of God to the oppressed workers of the world. If it means anything, it has to mean that they - even the wretchedly poor - can see their life transformed and know prosperity.

And that is why this topic is such a big deal: Jesus did indeed come to bring good news to the poor (and everyone else), but many of us go on under the entirely mistaken impression that He taught His disciples to embrace poverty.

I have certainly seen many Christians (and Christian leaders) react in a way which suggests that, to their way of thinking, anyone who questions the 'virtue of poverty' must be saying that Jesus wants us to embrace self-centred self-indulgence.

Well clearly, that can't be the case; Jesus is not promoting self-serving self-indulgence. One only need look at the Parable of the Rich Fool, in Luke 12:16-21. But the problem with the Rich Fool is that he thinks his wealth is 'all about him', **not** that he is prosperous.

He was planning years of well-funded retirement for himself, instead of asking God what assignment the provision enabled him to undertake.

Or as God says to him, when telling him his life ends that very night, "these things you have prepared, who are they for?" And that, Jesus tells us, is the fate of those who store up riches to themselves and not towards God.

But nowhere does Jesus tell us not to have money, even if we have somehow perceived that He did.

Secondly - God's Day of Vengeance is Good News for us. It is central to us being set free and made into a plantation of Yahweh, for the display of His glory.

What does this mean for me?

To put it bluntly, Satan prefers "keep them stupid" as his main strategy; but if he can't have that, then "keep them poor and struggling with their finances - and thinking this is normal" is the next best thing. As I will keep repeating, Satan can't keep you out of heaven but he would like to ensure that you remain ineffective with respect to overthrowing his current sovereignty. If he can get you to believe in the blessedness of poverty, his objective is pretty much accomplished.

So let's confront the lie. Ask yourself: 'how many people have I heard - including myself - saying at some point or other "I feel God is calling me to do such and such"?'

Now, how many of those have gone on to do just what they said God was calling them to do, and to do it **far more extensively** than they ever thought or imagined? (Which is how God's assignments always are intended to work: *"far more abundantly than all you could ask or imagine..."*)

And of those who **haven't** done what they said God called them to, how many times was it because they not only didn't find a way of accessing the financial resource necessary to realise that vision, but they never could get their own finances sorted out...?

It is useful to consider the implications of **inadvertently rejecting God's good intentions towards you**, with regard to money and financial resource. You wouldn't just be refusing your own opportunity to enjoy freedom and become fruitful in the Kingdom; you would also be putting yourself in the position of never being able to help **anyone else** break out of wretched poverty and enter into their assignment and inheritance in the Kingdom.

Finally, in case you have been thinking that we have been running two unrelated threads in this chapter - prosperity for the poor, and vengeance on God's enemy - I would argue that they absolutely do belong together.

The reason why it matters that we understand that God's Day of Vengeance is aimed at His enemy and ours (i.e. Satan), is this: we **really need to understand** that when any person comes into the fullness of the freedom, restoration, healing, prosperity and comfort which is already theirs in the Kingdom of God, **that** is Vengeance against God's enemy. You may not have understood that, but he totally gets it; and screams in futile, powerless rage.

Makes you think, doesn't it.

So, where to next?

Hopefully we are building some kind of agreement here, that maybe the things we thought we were seeing in the Gospels aren't quite making the case we thought they were; and maybe there is something positive around wealth that Jesus has more to say about than we realised.

But I know what you are thinking: "Blessed are the poor in spirit" (Matthew 5) and "Blessed are the poor" (Luke 6). It is time for us to tackle the Sermon on the Mount, and its parallel passage in Luke (sometimes called, the Sermon on the Plain).

Would you be surprised if I said all is not what it seems?

Chapter Seven: Blessed are the Beggars

Now when Jesus saw the crowds, he went up on a mountainside and sat down. His disciples came to him, and he began to teach them.

He said:

"Blessed are the poor in spirit, for theirs is the kingdom of heaven.
Blessed are those who mourn, for they will be comforted.
Blessed are the meek, for they will inherit the earth.
Blessed are those who hunger and thirst for righteousness, for they will be filled.
Blessed are the merciful, for they will be shown mercy.
Blessed are the pure in heart, for they will see God.
Blessed are the peacemakers, for they will be called children of God.
Blessed are those who are persecuted because of righteousness, for theirs is the kingdom of heaven.
Blessed are you when people insult you, persecute you and falsely say all kinds of evil against you because of me. Rejoice and be glad, because great is your reward in heaven, for in the same way they persecuted the prophets who were before you."

Matthew 5:1-12, NIV

What are we looking at here?

The Sermon on the Mount is arguably the best known "set piece" of Jesus' ministry; at the very least it is up there with the Feeding of the Five Thousand, the Garden of Gethsemane and Golgotha in terms of the place it holds in western culture. Whether it is in a U2 song, a political speech or a cartoon, people can recognise references to "The Sermon on the Mount" - even if they might struggle to quote any specific saying from it. For better or worse, The Sermon on the Mount is part of our cultural heritage.

It is not much different in the Church. Many biblical commentators have concluded that Matthew is presenting Jesus as the new and better Moses, and that the Sermon on the Mount, so called, is the parallel to Moses bringing the Law down to the people from Mount Sinai, with the nine Beatitudes as the counterpoint to the ten commandments of the Decalogue.

Therefore the Sermon as a whole presents us with the "new commandments" which we as Christians are to follow; and right at the beginning of the Sermon we have a statement that the poor (Luke) or the poor in spirit (Matthew) are blessed and that the Kingdom of Heaven is specifically reserved for them.

What's wrong with this picture?

I don't think this "new Mosaic Law" story stands up to examination.

It may however explain a phenomenon I feel I have observed over the decades; namely, that in most churches of my (rather wide) acquaintance, any given Sunday sermon is more likely to be preached on a passage from Romans and Galatians than on a passage from the Gospels.

My hypothesis would be this: if we think Jesus, in His teaching, was simply "raising the bar" with regards to the righteous demands of the Law; and doing so in order that, when He died and rose again, our deliverance would be even more striking; then, living as we do after His death and resurrection, His teaching to the Law-bound Jews is of little direct relevance to us as Believers.

I hope I am wrong in this perception, because it would seem to indicate a rather low regard for Jesus' understanding of His own assignment and mission. Would He devote so much effort to establishing something He would shortly make irrelevant?

The obvious alternative, if you think Jesus is being "the New Moses" here, is not much better; namely the thought that perhaps our faith really **is** all about compliance with a set of (impossibly demanding) legal requirements.

To both those possibilities I would simply reply, "No, Jesus is, as always, teaching us about the Kingdom and laying important foundations - but He also knows that most of His hearers will misunderstand what He is saying because, **at this point in time**, they lack the crucial key to understanding."

I will say more about this in the next chapter, but for now I simply mean that it really does matter that we read these chapters in Matthew (and Luke) correctly.

With regards to the content of the Beatitudes, I believe we have been making a fundamental error in the way we read them. However noble and well-intentioned the "bias to the poor" theology may have been, it is missing the point.

What Jesus actually says is very good news for all the groups He references, but not at all because God is building a collection of people who continue to have miserable lives.

What should we be seeing instead?

The so called Beatitudes are a record of Jesus training His disciples, firstly to see past "the mess people are now" and on to their destiny as Kingdom citizens; and secondly, to not be too upset when these future citizens of the Kingdom give them - the disciples - a hard time or run them out of town.

The passage itself makes it clear that Jesus was **not** preaching a sermon to a great multitude about the blessedness of various states. But we will need to unpack this in stages.

First of all, imagine that you are in an English class, and the teacher reads you Matthew 5:1-2

"Now when Jesus saw the crowds, he went up on a mountainside and sat down. His disciples came to him, and he began to teach them." (NIV)

She then asks, "according to this passage, who did Jesus teach?"

If you answer "the crowds", you get no marks. The correct answer is "Jesus taught the disciples."

If the teacher then asks, "according to the passage, where are the crowds?" the correct answer would be "we aren't told but can assume they are still down the hill somewhere, because the passage only says that Jesus went up on a mountainside and that the disciples came to him".

This is hardly rocket surgery: the point is to see what the passage actually says, not what we have always seen there, which may well have been "Jesus speaking from the mountainside to the crowd".

What about the next question that our imaginary English teacher might ask: "What can Jesus see; and what can the disciples see?"

Of course the passage doesn't tell us, and our English teacher might be exceeding her brief. But if you have ever sat on a mountainside or hillside, you should be able to work out the answer.

Generally speaking, if you sit on the side of a mountain or hill, you sit either a) with **your back to** the rising slope, that is, looking downhill; or b) you sit sideways on the hillside, looking across the slope, with a field of view roughly centred on the same elevation as you are at. You almost never sit *facing up* the mountainside; not unless rolling backwards, head over heels, is your thing. Sitting facing up the hillside, on even a very mild slope, is all but impossible to maintain.

So it is not a bad assumption to say that Jesus was sitting with his back to the mountain, facing downhill, and that his disciples were sitting beside, behind or in front of him, **facing the same way**; or possibly facing across towards him if they were out to the sides. If they were behind Him, they wouldn't be very far away, or His voice wouldn't reach them.

We can't tell from the text exactly how many disciples were here, whether it was just the Twelve or a somewhat larger group. (I think there are good internal reasons to think it was primarily the Twelve, newly appointed as Envoys - ἀπόστολοι, *'apostoloi'*). But we can tell that the immediate audience were disciples, as opposed to the general crowd - at least at the beginning.

The key conclusion is that they were mostly looking downhill, **and would therefore still be looking at the great crowds below them**.

In John 6:3-5 we read of a similar scenario:

Then Jesus went up on a mountainside and sat down with his disciples. The Jewish Passover Festival was near. When Jesus looked up and saw a great crowd coming toward him...

Jesus just **looked up**, not around, in order to see the crowd; He was facing a crowd downhill of Him. As one does, sitting on a hillside.

Back to Matthew 5: at this point in proceedings, Jesus is **speaking to his disciples** (not to the crowd); **but the crowd is very much in sight**.

In fact, by the end of Matthew 7, it is the crowd and their reaction to Jesus words (panic-stricken terror, not amazement) that we read about. So we know they came up the hill to gather around and listen, and probably quite early on (see the next chapter for just how early I think that was). But **at this stage**, Jesus is talking to His disciples; and the most obvious conclusion is that what He says next is **about the crowds** upon whom they are all gazing.

"Jesus began to teach them, saying: 'Blessed are the poor in spirit, for theirs is the kingdom of heaven.'" (Matt 5:3, NIV)

Well? Who is he talking about?

That is actually a rather important question. Is Jesus starting on a set of generalised statements about what is good and blessed? We certainly can read them that way, but they start sounding more like Platitudes than Beatitudes.

I didn't just accuse Jesus of speaking in platitudes; but I am wondering if we think He does. Would you try telling a genuinely destitute person that they are blessed because they are so poor? At the very least, you would want to be just as destitute as they are before you dared; and I am still not convinced you wouldn't get a deservedly angry response.

And while you consider that one, here's another question: what on earth does "the poor in spirit" (οἱ πτωχοὶ τῷ πνεύματι) mean, anyway?

As we have mentioned in an earlier chapter, *ptwchoi* ("πτωχοὶ") means "beggars", not "poor". Poor would most likely be *penhs* ("πένης"), from *penomai* ("πένομαι") 'to work for a living' i.e. as a day labourer, without resources other than their ability to work one day at a time - and from which we get the idea of "living in penury". This is the word used (as "πένησιν") in 2 Corinthians 9:9, "gifts to the poor". The root of *ptwchos*, a beggar, on the other hand, is *ptwssw* ("πτώσσω"), to shrink from, cringe or beg.

Pause a moment. "Blessed are those who cringe in spirit." Or "beg". Or "shrink back". Really?

It just isn't a very compelling idea. They are blessed **because they cringe**? That can't be right, surely.

Well, let's look at who Jesus is talking about in this way, and why. To do that it will help if we ask a seemingly unrelated question:

How did the disciples feel about crowds?

We know from the three Synoptic accounts (Matthew, Mark and Luke) of the feeding of the five thousand men that the disciples **at least** felt some responsibility for the crowds. There is more than a hint that they also saw them as a problem or a necessary evil.

"Send them away so they can find food" (and so that we don't end up with a big angry mob on our hands...)

Put yourself in the disciples' shoes for a moment. **You** are following Jesus because of an intimate encounter with the Messiah (He filled your boats with fish, He called you from your tax table, He saw you under your fig tree, or whatever). You want to be with Him every moment; but that doesn't stop you from feeling a bit **annoyed by the huge crowd** following Him - and you - everywhere you go, and giving you not a moment's peace.

If you also consider the words of the disciples when Jesus is pressed on all sides by the crowd during the healing of the woman with the issue of blood, or the disciples trying to prevent parents from bringing children to Jesus, you realise that the disciples weren't necessarily always shouting for joy at the appearance of yet another crowd. (As I said, put yourself in their shoes; maybe you just want Jesus to yourself, for a bit.)

Back to Matthew 5, how *do* the disciples feel about the crowd? They might be thinking, "fantastic, best crowd ever!"; but on the other hand, maybe one or two of them had said something like, 'look at them all; a field full of beggars, saying "give me, give me, give me."' That is entirely supposition on my part, but not improbable or unreasonable.

Possibly someone called them spiritual beggars; equally possibly, someone called them 'beggars in the wind', which would fit with a pleasantly breezy hillside above the Sea; and "οἱ πτωχοὶ τῷ πνεύματι" can mean the beggars in the wind just as easily as it means the beggars in the spirit. (*pneuma* - πνεύμα - means wind or breath before ever it means spirit, so we always need to ask ourselves if we are over-spiritualising the text when we translate every occurrence as if it *has to be* "spirit".) Perhaps it even has the sense of "the beggars whom the wind has blown in".

Whatever may have happened, Jesus sits with his disciples, looking down towards the crowds, and tells his disciples:

"These 'spiritual beggars' (or beggars in the wind) are blessed; the kingdom of the heavens is theirs. The ones who have come here wailing are blessed; they are going to be comforted. The ones who wouldn't say "boo" to a goose are blessed; they are going to take possession of the earth. The ones who are always demanding justice are blessed; they are going to be satisfied. The pitiful ones are blessed; they are going to be shown pity. The ones with "spotless hearts" are blessed; they are going to see God. The collaborators are blessed; they are going to be called sons of God. The ones on the run from justice are blessed, because theirs is the kingdom of the heavens."

I have deliberately chosen unfamiliar (but still entirely accurate) words to translate the first part of each statement. That is because I think it is important to understand that Jesus is not presenting spiritual archetypes, but rather describing an array of rather difficult and unattractive people.

We should be reading those referenced in the first 8 statements of the "Beatitudes" as starting from a rather 'negative' position. We have already looked at Beatitude One (The Poor in Spirit), who are actually the *ptwchoi* (beggars) in some detail, so what about the other seven groups?

Beatitude Two (Those Who Mourn):

πενθοῦντες are **those who wail**, hence **mourners**. We asked this in the previous chapter with regard to Isaiah 61, but let us ask again: what is the context here? Who would be a mourner or wailer?

Judea is under Roman occupation, and riven by internal faction fighting (which often included fighting of the non-metaphorical kind). Combined with what were clearly poor health outcomes (or else Jesus would never have had so many sick people to deal with), mourners could be bereft for both political and societal reasons.

In the kingdom of this world, how blessed is it to be a mourner? And how comforting is the comfort you do receive? Not very.

There is no comfort when your losses have no solution. But a mourner who enters the Kingdom of God? Different story. You stop being a victim. Your problems have solutions. You are the head and not the tail. Or as we saw in Chapter Three, "You tell it - storm, attack, illness, whatever - to stop".

Beatitude Three (The Meek):

πραεῖς are **the quiet, the meek and the soft**. Being meek in this kingdom (of the world) doesn't lead to being given possession of anything; it more regularly ends in being taken advantage of.

Of course there were many who flocked to Jesus because they needed hope. Jesus is not saying that being meek will help them; He is saying that in the Kingdom the formerly meek will be able to take possession of the world. (Which, please note, is nothing to do with overthrowing the Government.)

When Jesus later tells His followers to "turn the other cheek", that is an active posture, not an exhortation to become meek. I would advise caution before we accept the picture of "Gentle Jesus, meek and mild".

This is the Man who could call His disciples 'cowards' because they failed to stop a storm.

Beatitude Four (Those who Hunger and Thirst for Righteousness):

πεινῶντες καὶ διψῶντες τὴν δικαιοσύνην are those who **hunger and thirst** after - what? We say 'righteousness', because we have learnt to read this word this way in its theological sense, but it is fundamentally the upholding of what is right, justice and the fulfilling of law (or Law) - it also describes the work of a judge.

It would apply, for example, to the man who asked Jesus to force his brother to share the inheritance. Imagine someone waving a placard and shouting "Give me my rights; I demand justice!" The mental picture this conjures up may not be as sympathetic as "those who hunger and thirst after righteousness".

And Jesus makes a somewhat comic promise to explain how blessed they will be - using a word for cattle eating their fill and being fattened up. So one can read this as "those who think they are pursuing their rights and their due are blessed because in the Kingdom they will finally really be filled with good things - like satisfied cattle."

People may have come to Jesus in the hope He would stop their neighbour encroaching on their land, or force the landlord to do something about the drains; but that isn't **why** they are blessed.

The kingdom of this world may be one big zero-sum game, so in order for me to win, you have to lose; but in the Kingdom of the Heavens, everyone gets a double portion.

Beatitude Five (The Merciful):

ἐλεήμονες are either the **pitiful** (as in my rendering above) or the **merciful**. So either blessed are the pitiful for they will be shown pity; or blessed are the merciful, for they shall be shown mercy.

And despite the way I rendered it earlier in this chapter (mostly to break the tyranny of the familiar), I suspect "merciful" is the correct rendering; but not because of how we have been hearing that word all along. It isn't necessarily nice.

Given the pattern of the other beatitudes is "blessed are the [insert moral or practical weakness here]", then ἐλεήμονες could cover those who tell you they are being merciful to you, when in fact by doing so, they are asserting their power or superiority over you.

For example, Calypso uses this same Greek term to tell Odysseus that she, Calypso, is merciful, when the reality is that she has held him captive for years, and shown him no mercy at all, only lust. (Hom. Od. 5.191).

Closer to home, "you owe me money but I shall be merciful" sounds like something a Pharisee could say. Or perhaps it is more this: mercy implies rights or penalties not enforced; it doesn't necessarily extend to fixing the other person's problem.

I don't insist on any of these readings, but mercy without compassion or practical action is not a posture proper to men and women, when we see our own need for God's mercy - which is both compassionate and practical.

Beatitude Six (The Pure in Heart):

καθαροὶ τῇ καρδίᾳ are the **pure, cleansed or spotless in heart.**
The obvious response is that people who are self-consciously "pure
in heart" can be pretty uncomfortable to be around (the sense of
humour is usually the first thing to be removed, which is what the
root of καθαροὶ is about - carrying off or pruning).

Furthermore, as Jeremiah noted (17:9), "the heart is deceitful above
all things"; so who can say of themselves that they have a pure
heart?

But the good news for those suffering from self-righteousness is that
in the Kingdom they will finally see God. No one sees God and still
thinks that they, themselves, are pure; the blessing of the Kingdom
is to see God and realise that you are loved and accepted by, and
sharing in, His Goodness.

Beatitude Seven (The Peacemakers):

εἰρηνοποιοί are **those who make peace.** Israel at this time is subject
to Roman rule. So by those who make peace we actually mean...
that's right: collaborators.

Tax-farmers were a specific case within this, but many business men
and anyone operating within a political role had to be balancing
their loyalty to the nation with their commitment to their own
prosperity or success, and erring in favour of the foreign overlords.

If it was left to human judgement, it would be the zealots and
revolutionaries who were labelled "Sons of God", on account of
their devotion to the national identity and interest (as they saw it).

In the Kingdom, those who have hitherto compromised their
consciences - or even just surrendered to the inevitability of Roman
overlordship - can find their calling as true children of God.

Beatitude Eight (Those who are Persecuted because of Righteousness):

δεδιωγμένοι ἕνεκεν δικαιοσύνης are **those who have been pursued**, or otherwise set in motion, **because of justice.**[1]

We've been reading this as a description of believers being persecuted, but this sounds more like gangsters or bank robbers, on the run because of justice. (Ouch!)

Or it could be those who are simply marching to the beat of a different drummer (i.e. a non-Roman one, and therefore having to run away so as not to suffer interrogation as "a person of interest to the authorities").

And yet, those on the run because of justice can have the same inheritance as the blessed beggars: access to - possession of, even - the Kingdom of the Heavens.

Before we tackle the last "beatitude", a pause for breath. I quite understand if you are baulking at an "alternative reading" of this very familiar passage. And of course, most of these terms **could** be taken in a (somewhat) positive light. There are just two massive obstacles to this "traditional" view, and you need to be able to address them if you want to keep with the well-trodden path.

One, if these are all positive, how do you read "blessed are the cringing beggars of the Spirit (or in the wind)" in a positive light?

And the other is what Jesus says in the final "blessed". Because the focus changes from the crowd to the disciples themselves: "And blessed are you when **they** reproach you and pursue you and speak all kinds of good-for-nothing things against you falsely for My sake.

---

[1] *There is a whole book to write on why translating διώκω as "persecute" is such a dubious practice. It means "cause to run, chase, hunt, set in quick motion". If someone chases you out of town, is that persecution?*

Be glad and rejoice exceedingly because your recompense is great in the heavens; for thus they pursued the prophets who were before you."

Who is "they"? Jesus doesn't (despite suggestions in the NIV and elsewhere to the contrary) say "people" or "men" here. He says "they".

The most obvious "they" in terms of the sense of the passage is obvious. It is: the beggars, the wailers, the softies, the activists, the collaborators and all. The crowd "upon whom we are gazing." Yes, them.

What does this mean?

My impression is that we have mostly been reading this passage as if it said "people like this are blessed - because they are like this, i.e. wretched." So poor people are blessed because they are poor, mourners are blessed because they are mourners, meek people are blessed because they are meek, and so on. But I don't think we really believe that, nor should we; and certainly not that beggars are blessed because they are beggars.

These people are blessed because, whatever has brought them here today - a jumble of emotions and needs and good intentions, even - the Kingdom of the heavens has a much better future in store for them.

What I am suggesting is that Jesus is **not at all** telling those who follow him to become beggars, mourners, meek - let alone persecuted. *He is telling His disciples the kind of people who they will be ministering to*, because these are the people who are drawn to Jesus, and who have a Kingdom destiny.

In other words, "you have been seeing a crowd - and a problem, or even an annoyance. But if you are going to follow me in this work, you need to start seeing them the way I do. Don't see the problem or the pain: *see the destiny!*"

In the process of telling the disciples to focus on "what is to come" - if my guess about what might have already been murmured is correct - Jesus is also gently rebuking them for the wrong judgements they have been making.

To put all of this in the simplest terms, we have been making a big mistake when we read the Sermon on the Mount. We read "Blessed are the poor because they are poor"; Jesus says "maybe they are spiritual beggars, but they are blessed because they aren't staying like this; they have a Kingdom to inherit!"

And it is at least possible that Jesus is using humour in the final "blessed". Something like this: "if you boys have been finding the crowds annoying so far, I have good news: they will chase you out of town too - and you can rejoice in that because they chased the prophets before you, and there is a great payday in heaven for you also..." All slightly tongue in cheek. But the point Jesus is making is that blessing can look like something else - and be pretty messy, with it - when you are just starting out or are mid-process.

Hebrews 12 captures this "focusing on the destiny" well. At the point where Jesus went to the cross, He wasn't able to say "I have twelve associates who are super-smart and totally dialled in to everything I have been teaching them, and a wider audience who are fully bought in to my message."

But as the writer of Hebrews says of Him, "**on account of the joy set before Him**, He suffered the cross, despised its indignity and is seated at the right hand of the Throne of God". Jesus knew His disciples would get it fully in the end, and be His witnesses and make disciples, because He already knew how the story ends: with a great host "which no man could number, from every nation and tribe and people and tongue, standing before the throne..." (Rev 7:9)

Was the cross and its shame a big deal? We can't even begin to imagine; but the joy of the destiny was much, much greater.

In other words, the Plan (God's Plan) has some real personal cost involved. But you can't judge whether it is working, based on how smooth the path seems, or how gracious those you are helping are.

It is the Plan, stick with it.

What does this mean for me?

Hopefully this is obvious. If you have held back from believing that God wants to bless you financially or in your health or in any other practical aspect of life, because you have a sneaking suspicion that He actually likes His people to be penniless and in mourning, **that is nowhere in Scripture** - and certainly not here.

Quite the opposite - whether your problem is your terrible circumstances or your self-centredness or your self-righteousness, God's Kingdom is bigger than all of those and as far as God is concerned, it is all yours.

Secondly, if you are already on God's team and trying to understand how to find people who will respond to the Gospel, He is saying to you "don't be put off by how annoying or awkward or wretched people are: seen through the perspective of what the Kingdom is, **they are blessed**. You just need to walk - and sometimes run - with God's plan, in order to help them get there."

This should be super-encouraging. Jesus is affirming that the Kingdom is strong enough to receive and transform anyone, regardless of what a mess they are in to start with, and despite the trouble they may cause along the way.

Whether you see yourself in the crowd, or amongst the disciples already, that is extremely Good News.

So, where to next?

We have only dealt with the first few verses of the three chapters given to "the Sermon on the Mount" so far, and as I have suggested, it is clear Jesus begins by giving some core training to His disciples.

But what happens when the crowd comes up the hill to find Him? Presumably He tells them just how blessed they are…?

Chapter Eight: A Pinch of Salt

"You are the salt of the earth. But if the salt loses its saltiness, how can it be made salty again? It is no longer good for anything, except to be thrown out and trampled underfoot."

"You are the light of the world. A town built on a hill cannot be hidden. Neither do people light a lamp and put it under a bowl. Instead they put it on its stand, and it gives light to everyone in the house."

"In the same way, let your light shine before others, that they may see your good deeds and glorify your Father in heaven."
Matthew 5:13-16, NIV

What are we looking at here?

Jesus shares two parabolic metaphors to encourage His hearers to be salt and light in the world.

The first of these has caused commentators some problems, since the table salt we know is pretty salty whatever you do to it; but someone eventually suggested that the mineral salt of the Middle East was actually a conglomeration of other crystalline minerals along with the sodium chloride we know as salt, and so the salt could be leached out leaving only the other (tasteless? bad-tasting?) minerals behind.

These two motifs of Christians as salt and light are amongst the most powerful images we have in the Gospels.

What's wrong with this picture?

There is a huge problem in the Greek of v.13, namely that it simply **can't** mean what the English translations all say it does. By the time we have uncovered what it does mean, and considered the context, we will realise that Jesus was not describing the virtues of a believer, but rather confronting Israel with its failure to live up even to its own marketing hype - let alone the Covenant whose benefits they should have been enjoying.

The problem is that if we read this incorrectly, then we will create a huge stumbling-block for ourselves in the rest of Matthew chapters 5, 6 and 7.

Jesus deliberately dismays His hearers by confronting them with their failure and then telling them the standards they need to live up to - without ever disclosing to them the secret of the Kingdom. He isn't being heartless, but He is giving them some ballast to carry, in order to prevent an outbreak that could get them all killed.

What should we be seeing instead?

If you have read Chapter Seven ("Blessed are the Beggars"), you will know that, at the beginning of the passage usually referred to as "the Sermon on the Mount", Matthew clearly states that Jesus is speaking just to His disciples (verses 5:1-2). At the end, (Matthew 7:28), Matthew states with equal clarity that the crowds have been listening to His teaching (and are scared by it!)

So: at what point do the crowds start listening in?

Since the text doesn't tell us, we have to make a judgement based on how we read the text and its probable context. My own conclusion is that from this point onwards (Matthew 5:13), the crowds (or at least the first wave) have made it up the hill and are gathering around Jesus and the disciples where they are seated. How long does it take to notice that the man you came to hear has moved a little way up the hill? About as long as it takes for Jesus to give His disciples their briefing on seeing the crowd differently...

From this point onwards, therefore, Jesus is clearly **speaking to the** crowd, and He is speaking to them **as the Jewish nation**.

Firstly, Jesus gives two figures, one about salt and the other, slightly more extended, about light. In the English versions they seem innocuous, and not particularly oriented to a specific audience.

Once we read them correctly we will see a much stronger narrative: as God's Covenant People, the Jews should be the one group of people on earth who actually a) **understand what is going on in this fallen world** and who b) **model the Goodness of God**. Instead, they have rather lost the plot, and their "fine works" won't stand up to even the most cursory scrutiny.

After these two figures, Jesus embarks upon an extended dissertation on the Law: how He has not come to abolish the Law but to fulfil it, and how that plays out in practice (e.g. it isn't just committing adultery that is wrong, but looking with lust in your heart, and so on). And He deliberately withholds the one piece of information which could turn this picture from "a more terrifying version of the Law's demands" into a picture of the Kingdom, where God Himself will make fulfilling the spirit of the Law accessible and possible for all people.

If we fail to read this correctly, then we become tangled in the apparent 'tension' between the content of this passage and the rest of Jesus' teaching - not to mention the potential conflict with, for example, the Pauline Epistles, with regard to whether or not we need to keep the Mosaic Law.

So to summarise, Jesus is not addressing His disciples any more, and those He addresses He treats as representative of their specific nation, Israel. He is not speaking to a global, multi-ethnic 'everyman'; but neither is He giving the crowd a new Mosaic Law to follow.

Before we look at the figures of salt and light, let us step back and consider the context once more, because there is one more factor in play, here: **the danger of having so many people in a potentially highly volatile setting**.

As the end of Matthew 4 makes plain, the crowds around Jesus ("many crowds", says the Greek) came from "Syria..., Galilee, the Decapolis, Jerusalem, Judea and the region across the Jordan."

This is a very large catchment, even if those coming from Syria only included people from Tyre and Sidon, the part of that Roman province which was closest to Judea. "Many crowds" suggests that a) there were a very large number of people and b) that they were in numerous, probably distinct, clusters.

It is useful to ask the question, "if I was Jesus, what would I do in this situation?" Most of us would answer something to the effect that it was a fantastic opportunity to get His message out to a very wide audience; which only goes to show, once again, that Jesus was **very clear about**, and focussed on, **His assignment**, in a way that most of us are not.

As we noted in the earlier chapter, Jesus has just given the disciples a briefing on how to see the crowds as He Himself does. "Blessed are the beggars in the Spirit (or Wind), for theirs is the Kingdom of the Heavens." In other words, don't see the problem, **see the destiny**.

And yet: Jesus does not - **at this point** - give those beggars in the wind the secret of the Kingdom. (Which is perhaps why it was so important that He briefed the disciples for their future ministry; He was relying on **them** to lead people into their destiny when the time was right).

On the contrary: while everything He says to them is the truth (of course), it is deliberately **not** the **whole** truth.

Far from releasing them into their Kingdom destiny, Jesus claps a stopper over their enthusiasm. It is a deliberate act, and when He has finished,

ἐξεπλήσσοντο οἱ ὄχλοι ἐπὶ τῇ διδαχῇ αὐτοῦ.

That is, the crowds were panic-stricken (or overwhelmed in a negative sense) at His teaching.

Why does Jesus do this?

The answer is relatively simple. He has attracted huge numbers of people, from two Roman provinces and from a host of administrative districts. For example, the Decapolis was not under Herod's rule, although Jerusalem and Judea were, even though all three were part of the province of Judea.

In other words, all the political administrators for miles around might be interested in anything arising from this gathering of crowds. Not for the last time, Jesus is facing the very real possibility of inadvertently sparking a revolt; and **inciting a revolt plays no part in His assignment**.

The Kingdom is most definitely for these crowds, and yet if He introduces them to its secret **at this point**, the most likely outcome is that they a) fail to understand and b) take things into their own hands. Rome has already put down numerous rebellions against its rule, and stands forever ready to do the same again.

The **disciples** still don't understand the nature of the Kingdom (as evidenced by their questions about when Jesus will restore the Kingdom to Israel, much later on in the Gospels), so Jesus could hardly expect the freshly-arrived **crowds** to "get it".

In Jesus' place, others might have chosen to "make the most of" both the moment and the crowd, and then publicly regretted whatever happened next (while pointing out that they, themselves, had done nothing wrong). Jesus, however, is not a populist preacher; He is a man on a very specific assignment.

So instead of allowing any possibility of an eruption of "Kingdom-mania", He provokes the crowd (perhaps rather as this present book is attempting to do), not to rebellion but to fruitful puzzlement and even dismay.

This provocation is all of a piece with His parables elsewhere: He casts fundamentally Good News in a format which cuts straight across the mindset and expectations of His hearers, and leaves them more at sea than ever. Only with the (missing) key will they, for example, ever understand how their righteousness can be greater than that of the scribes and Pharisees.

He talks about salt and light, and does so in terms that clearly reference the Jewish nation, rather than His twelve new envoys (apostles).

The first clue is the structure He uses, namely "you are the x of the earth / world". This does not fit well with an address to His inner circle. The apostles do not stand as actors on the world stage; that is where **nations and tribes** stand.

Let me give you an equivalent statement: "you are the world leader in heavy industry". In this instance who is "you"? In other words, who are we speaking about? It could be a nation, e.g. "China is the world leader in heavy industry"; it could be a company, e.g. "Hyundai is the world leader in heavy industry". But it is unlikely to be an individual, not even the CEO of a large conglomerate.

"Fred is the world leader in heavy industry" is just bad English - we either mean that he is the foremost leader in the world of heavy industrial production, or that the company he leads is the world leader in heavy industry, in which case we should say so; but unless we are suggesting that Fred **personally** builds more ships and assembles more industrial equipment than any company or country does, he does not belong in that sentence.

I would argue that, in the same way, the "you" of "you are the salt of the earth" or "you are the light of the world" is more likely to be the nation of Israel, rather than the disciples.

That may not seem definitive to you, but there are two other major clues. "A city situated on the upper side of a mountain cannot be hidden by scraping earth over it" in Matthew 5:14 sounds - once we have translated the Greek literally instead of loosely - a lot like Jerusalem, the heart and embodiment of the Jewish nation. It doesn't sound like the disciples.

Secondly, "trampled underfoot by men" in Matthew 5:13 had been Israel's (and Jerusalem's) fate before, and, as Jesus knew only too well, would be so again. Jesus never suggested to the disciples that such could be **their** fate; but He does warn Israel repeatedly of what awaits **them**.

We also know from the testimony of a well-trained Pharisee that this "you are the x of the y" pattern was mirrored in the self-talk of the religious Jew. In Romans 2:17ff, and no doubt speaking from his own experience, Paul writes:

> *Now you, if you call yourself a Jew; if you rely on the law and boast in God; if you know his will and approve of what is superior because you are instructed by the law; if you are convinced that you are a guide for the blind,* ***a light for those who are in the dark****, an* ***instructor of the foolish****, a teacher of little children, because you have in the law the embodiment of knowledge and truth...*

> **(NIV, emphasis mine)**

So let us consider the figures of salt and light, one at a time.

When you look at the Greek of Matthew 5:13, it becomes immediately apparent that Jesus is using humour to make what might otherwise be a rather offensive observation. It all starts with the recognition that in Greek, as in Latin, "salt" is an everyday metaphor for "wit", meaning "sharp intelligence, often expressed with mordant humour as well as insight".

It goes like this (from the hearer's perspective):

"You are the salt of the earth"

(so far so good, and yes this is Israel's self narrative)

"But if salt should become foolish (μωραίνω)..."

(oh, hold on - salt can't become foolish, so Jesus is using ἅλας, salt, in its metaphorical sense of "wit, insight and understanding"; so we need to backtrack: "You are the source of understanding in the world, but if understanding becomes foolish...")

"...how can it be..."

And here is the crux of Jesus' own play on words: ἁλισθήσεται can be read as two homonyms (words identical in spelling and pronunciation, but with different meanings), meaning, respectively:

"...gathered together (of wits)"; AND *"made salty (of food)"*

So Jesus uses ἁλισθήσεται to say both "how can your wits be gathered?" and "how can your salt be made salty again?"[1]

---

[1] *The point I'm making is, since μωραίνω can only mean "become foolish", we must be talking about wit and wisdom, and not salt. I'm sure someone will quote my favourite Lexicon on the definition of μωραίνω, but I would cite this as a classic case of the way mistakes by translators then infect dictionaries via a process of circular reasoning. So yes, even Liddell and Scott appends 'to become insipid, "ἐὰν τὸ ἅλας μωρανθῇ" Ev.Matt.5.13' to its otherwise perfectly good entry for μωραίνω. There is no possibility that this is correct. Matt.5:13 is the only place in the entire canon of Greek literature where it has ever been suggested that μωραίνω means "become insipid" (let alone, "lose its saltiness") instead of the correct meaning, namely "become foolish". But if you fail to see the play on words around ἅλας, then you are left scrabbling for a meaning that could possibly fit.*

What is Jesus saying?

"You - Israel - are meant to be the insight and wisdom of the earth (implication: just like salt, making life bearable for everyone, not just yourselves). But if your wits are scattered, and your wisdom becomes foolishness, how can you get that back?" The answer goes on: "there is no value left in you except to be thrown outside and trampled underfoot by men."

What starts as a clever multi-layered pun has a sting in its tail. You can imagine the faces of the crowd, caught between laughing and grimacing.

Now, we know (or we should) that Jesus isn't being unkind. The warning is very real, and soon to be realised, with the revolt of AD66 culminating with the destruction of the Temple in AD70 and the subsequent removal of all references to the Jews in the former land of Israel. (By the second Century, even the Roman Province of Judea was disestablished and its lands combined with Syria to become the enlarged Province of Syria-Palaestina.)

But from our perspective, we also know that the promise of the Father is coming, namely that His Spirit will indwell His people in His Kingdom. We could say, "God's Spirit living in you and guiding you? You can't get more insight and wisdom than that..."

So the wits can, in fact, be gathered and the salt made salty; **but that is a truth and a secret which is not being shared with the crowds today**.

When Jesus talks about light, we see a similar pattern.

"You are the light of the world [order]."

κόσμος (*kosmos*) is primarily the world as order, as opposed to χάος (*chaos*), and this is important both because God created the world to have order, and because the enemy has corrupted the world to follow his own perverse order.

> *"A city situated on the upper side of a mountain cannot be hidden under a covering of earth. Neither does anyone kindle a lamp and then place it under a bucket, but rather on a lampstand, and it lights all those in the house."*

Jesus uses the same Greek word - λυχνίαν - as is used in the LXX in Ex25:30 (v 31 in the English Bibles) for the lampstand of the sanctuary.

The reference could be deliberate, i.e. "ever wondered why the lampstand is in the sanctuary? It symbolised Israel's role in the world." The word in the Hebrew version of Exodus is מְנוֹרָה or *menorah* - which simply means lampstand.

Which all sounds reasonable and encouraging, but here is the kicker:

> *"So - **shine** your light before the face of [all] men, so that they may see your **fine** works, and glorify your Father in the heavens."*

> ***(Emphasis mine)***

Once again we need to reflect on the context. Jesus is speaking to a defeated, divided, subject people, who may, through the private practice of piety, convince themselves that they are honouring God with their lives; but Jesus confronts them with a very inconvenient truth: you can't hide Jerusalem (and all its mess and poverty and brokenness); and yet you, Israel, are meant to be the light of the world.

λαμψάτω is the 3rd singular aorist imperative, the clear implication of which is "let it shine, once, right now"; and specifically **not** "whenever you can, let it shine".

So the implication is "You are the light of the world? Great. So, go on, let's have a look at Jerusalem; **shine** some light on that right now, and let everyone see your καλὰ ἔργα, your fine works, and let them glorify your Father in heaven."

Or is that going to be a little awkward and uncomfortable?

And yes, καλὰ - *kala* - or "fine" has exactly the same ironic potential in Greek as it does in English.

I realise this may come as a shock: like me, you may have heard "let your light so shine before men that they may see your good works and glorify your Father in heaven" as a comforting benediction sending you on your way at the end of a Church service. But the context suggests that Jesus was saying something quite different.

He is using a little gentle irony to reflect back to them just how big a mess they are in. As Hebrews tells us, the old Covenant could never set anyone free, but it did present a shadow of the good things to come. Israel could have been enjoying the blessings of "the shadow", but even that they have fallen short of.

And while His hearers are completely off-balance, He hits them with another surprise:

"Don't think that I have come to abolish the Law and the Prophets!"

That was, of course, precisely what at least some of them were hoping for; some relief from the oppression of religion. Jesus instead, in the two and a half chapters that follow, unpacks examples of the teaching of the Law and the Prophets, identifies a much higher standard required for their fulfilment, and ties these higher standards to status in the Kingdom of Heaven.

By the end the crowd are, as I mentioned earlier, **panic-stricken or thrown off balance by His teaching**.

To be honest, in the past it had pretty much the same effect on me.

Jesus has told them absolutely everything - except this one thing: the secret of the Kingdom of the Heavens.

Without that secret - the promise that God Himself will indwell us, remove sin and make keeping His commands "what comes naturally" - what Jesus has shared sounds like **very bad news indeed**.

It is like training for the Olympic high jump for months and years and then being told on your way across the Olympic stadium that the bar will start at 100m high.

Whereas the secret of the Kingdom is like discovering that you are no longer subject to gravity - at which point 100m in the high jump is no big deal!

No wonder the crowd were terrified and not inclined to start anything disruptive.

What does this mean?

So what? Why include this chapter in a book about seeing the Kingdom of God? If we are not to be salt and light after all, then this seems kind of negative.

It's simple, really. The Sermon on the Mount has been used to "prove" so many things in direct opposition to **the Kingdom as it really is**, that we need to allow God to show us what is actually there.

Otherwise we find ourselves convinced that being poor would be more blessed than whatever we are, and that God's standards are so high that we might as well accept that our lives will be just one big failure after another, but - thank God - with forgiveness as the free door-pass to the after(life) party.

And that is a lie. God has success and prosperity in mind for **you**, just as He promised Abram:

> *I will make you into a great nation,*
> *and **I will bless you**;*
> *I will make your name great,*
> *and **you will be a blessing**.*
> *I will bless those who bless you,*
> *and whoever curses you I will curse;*
> *and **all peoples on earth***
> ***will be blessed through you**.*

> *(Genesis 12:2-3,NIV, emphasis mine)*

See the Kingdom. God wants to bless you, make you a blessing and bless nations through you.

Furthermore - and even I find this hard to let go of, so central has it been to my schooling from when I was five years old, and onwards - those pictures of salt and light are not going to help us live out our assignment in the Kingdom.

For example, many have used the motif of salt to suggest that the Church is a preservative that stops 'the meat of the world' from rotting. But that is the wrong picture.

Our job is not preserving the kingdom of this world system, it is that we should be those who [literally!] **earth** the Kingdom of Heaven: free captives; heal the sick; make disciples who are taught to observe as commands everything Jesus taught us; and so on.

Please don't misunderstand me: we should do all we can to defend the defenceless and prevent injustice in this world, but we know that only the Kingdom of the Heavens can provide actual answers for them.

Do we bring light? Yes, absolutely. But are we shining our light so that people will see our fine works? Or so that they see the one road that leads to the Father's household?

Jesus was holding up His own people's self-talk and using it to dismay them. We mustn't misunderstand and take on that unhelpful narrative as if it was the story of the Kingdom.

That still doesn't answer the question about whether this has been a slightly negative exercise. In every other chapter, once we have cleared away the misperceptions, there has been a really positive message to see: so what is the positive message here?

We probably have to step back and look again. Israel had a covenant with God. We tend to go straight to "the Law" when we mention covenant, but in fact the covenant is cut with Abram, before the Law was ever given.

The covenant promises - and delivers - good things. A wandering herdsman and his descendants inherit land, including houses and cities they didn't build and vineyards they didn't plant. Ultimately, of course, that covenant delivers Jesus the Messiah; and a better covenant, sealed and delivered with His blood.

Jesus isn't pointing back to the Law as the answer to their problems; but He is challenging the notion that they should be satisfied with what they are experiencing.

It is only religious pride that has them thinking in terms of being the salt of the earth and the light of the world. Being satisfied is the biggest hindrance to experiencing all that God has for us; so perhaps we should hear these two figures of salt and light as Jesus challenging their complacency; "if you are happy with yourselves when your reality falls so far short of the fantastic covenant you already have, how can I talk to you about the Kingdom of God?"

Sometimes, a bit of a shake-up is the most positive thing you can receive.

What does this mean for me?

I do absolutely understand how disconcerting it can be to drop a paradigm, let alone one which we thought was bringing comfort. Changing gears from fifth to reverse without stopping first or using the clutch doesn't come close.

Yes, it hurts - but not as much as **finishing** the journey, only to discover you were headed the wrong way, throughout.

There is nothing stopping us from applying the two figures Jesus uses, to ourselves, now that we understand what He was really saying. For example: when people speak to us, are they able to access the insight and wisdom of the Kingdom of God, or do they just tap into useless foolishness? The test is not whether we think we know a lot of spiritual truth, but rather what it is that people see in the light that we do have - do they see the Kingdom modelled and walked out in such a way that people are saying "wow, I want that too!"; or do they just see a big mess because we haven't got our own lives sorted out?

This is really about the impossibility of any accommodation between a religious mindset and the Kingdom of God; which as it happens, will also be the subject of our next and final chapter.

We have been running into this, throughout this book: things we thought were okay and true to say or believe, and which actually steal our life. *"Oh well, God knows what He is doing..." "It is up to God now..." "Bless us, but not too much..."*

If those still sound reasonable things to say, then you haven't yet seen the Kingdom. When you do, they will provoke a very different reaction!

So, where to next?

In the next, and final, chapter, we will look at the model that Jesus gave for the growth of the Kingdom. It doesn't involve preserving rotting meat, nor showing off our good works before the world. It is kind of below the radar. In fact, you would need a microscope to really see what is going on.

But first, it is time for another boat ride. The weather is better this time, but the disciples forget to bring any sandwiches...

Chapter Nine: A Touch of Leaven

The Pharisees and Sadducees came to Jesus and tested him by asking him to show them a sign from heaven.

He replied, "When evening comes, you say, 'It will be fair weather, for the sky is red,' and in the morning, 'Today it will be stormy, for the sky is red and overcast.' You know how to interpret the appearance of the sky, but you cannot interpret the signs of the times. A wicked and adulterous generation looks for a sign, but none will be given it except the sign of Jonah." Jesus then left them and went away.

When they went across the lake, the disciples forgot to take bread. "Be careful," Jesus said to them. "Be on your guard against the yeast of the Pharisees and Sadducees."

They discussed this among themselves and said, "It is because we didn't bring any bread."

Aware of their discussion, Jesus asked, "You of little faith, why are you talking among yourselves about having no bread? Do you still not understand? Don't you remember the five loaves for the five thousand, and how many basketfuls you gathered? Or the seven loaves for the four thousand, and how many basketfuls you gathered? How is it you don't understand that I was not talking to you about bread? But be on your guard against the yeast of the Pharisees and Sadducees." Then they understood that he was not telling them to guard against the yeast used in bread, but against the teaching of the Pharisees and Sadducees.

Matthew 16:1-12, NIV

What are we looking at here?

The Pharisees and Sadducees try to outsmart Jesus, and get outsmarted themselves, yet again. What can we learn? Well, that

Jesus really doesn't like Pharisees (or Sadducees), does He? He mocks them and warns His disciples against their teachings. Move along, nothing new to see here...

What's wrong with this picture?

Jesus didn't dislike people. In the case of the Pharisees and Sadducees, however, He recognised that they were so heavily invested in their own religious system, that they would never be able to accept the Kingdom of God.

If they didn't first repent of their existing mindset, they would inevitably try to subsume the Good News of the Kingdom into their own religious system; and that was never going to be an option. (You know the parables - new cloaks and old, new wine and old wineskins.) That is why He always refused to dialogue with them.

Instead He would make statements or pose questions which directly challenged their whole frame of reference - since only by "letting go" of that frame of reference could they ever see the Kingdom.

Of greater concern to Jesus was this: if His disciples were ever to take on board the religious mindset of the Pharisees or Sadducees, then they would be **unable to continue on in the Kingdom**.

What should we be seeing instead?

This passage contains what is arguably the most ignored commandment in the Bible (or perhaps the commandment which is most ignored because very few ever noticed it is there in the first place).

It also contains another great example of Jesus' sense of humour, a genuinely helpful piece of wisdom for the Pharisees and Sadducees, and the underlining of a fundamental principle of the Kingdom of God for the disciples.

What does this mean?

Let's start with the interaction with the Pharisees and Sadducees.

It actually runs in parallel to Jesus' conversation with that other Pharisee, Nicodemus, in John 3:1 onwards. There Nicodemus thinks he is paying Jesus a compliment by saying "we know you are a teacher who has come from God, for no-one could perform the signs you are doing if God were not with him." And Jesus, in effect, replies: "You haven't got a clue what you are talking about - because you cannot see the Kingdom of God."

Notice that "signs" are a key element of both interactions (here in Matthew 16 and in John 3). The fundamental issue between Jesus and the Pharisees is this: the Pharisees (think they) know that they **are** the definition of Godly righteousness, and are disturbed by "signs" which are wrought by anyone who is outside of their inner circle.

And there are clues in the Gospels that there **were** "signs" of a more approved nature, i.e. done by members of the religious establishment - for example when Jesus asks (in Matthew 12:27 and Luke 11:19) "then by whom do your sons cast them out?", referring to the casting out of evil spirits.

In other words, Pharisees **were** casting out evil spirits, themselves. (If that troubles you, it shouldn't; we don't know exactly how effective they were, but Israel's covenant relationship with God certainly gave them the authority to do this.)

Jesus on the other hand has nothing invested in the preservation of the religious *status quo*; He is bringing the Kingdom of the Heavens to bear on earth.

The Pharisees are reacting to what they see as "signs". They want to be able to pin them down and bring them under their own seal of approval (or otherwise). To Jesus these "signs" are simply the life of the Kingdom.

If you want to understand the commandment Jesus issues a few verses later, it is precisely because there is no possible accommodation between the Kingdom of God, on the one hand; and the religious system of approvals and disapprovals, in-group and out-group, merit and demerit of the Pharisees, on the other. The Pharisees want to be in control of everything, including signs; the Kingdom is simply not available to be appropriated by any human clique or authority, past or present.

I have little doubt that the Pharisees were, at least somewhat, genuine in their request that Jesus should "exhibit to them as a specimen, a sign from the heavens" (σημεῖον ἐκ τοῦ οὐρανοῦ ἐπιδεῖξαι αὐτοῖς).

Given their contentious relationship with the Sadducees ("who say there is no resurrection"), their request may well have been heartfelt, or at least a bet each way: "if He shows us an impressive sign, the Sadducees will have to admit that God's power is a real and present thing; and if He shows us a cheap conjuring trick, we catch Him out at last..."

Unfortunately Jesus is not at home to giving demonstrations on demand from those who have no understanding at all. "Give you an example of a sign from the heavens? Sure: 'Red sky at night, shepherd's delight; red sky at dawning, shepherd's warning!' Will that do you?"

Personally I find that hilarious; and of course Jesus is not being flippant, because He swings in behind the humour and turns the joke into a pretty sharp harpoon. "That's your problem, of course - you can read the weather in the heavens, but for all your talk about 'signs', you have no idea how to read the very clear signs of the times."

So what did Jesus mean by signs of the times? Without going into endless speculation, there are two sets of signs the Pharisees should have been reading.

Firstly, Israel was in a state of deep defeat and shame. The nation's downward journey had long since reached the point where only two tribes, Judah and Benjamin (plus a handful of Levites) were still in the Promised Land; and once again, they were under the heel of a pagan Empire, in this case Rome (Judea was a Roman province).

So even if Judah hadn't been a seething pot of the disaffected, the collaborators and the oppressed, the Pharisees should have realised something was lacking despite their religious self-satisfaction, since the nation was clearly not enjoying "the blessing of God".

Secondly, Jesus had been demonstrating that the Kingdom of God was at hand, and had arrived, all over Judea. And not only Jesus: He sent His disciples out before Him, and they too were demonstrating the reality of the Kingdom. Surely this was also a sign; and specifically a sign that they, the Pharisees, were riding the wrong horse.

Which brings us to the helpful advice. Jesus told them that it was the hallmark of a wretched and adulterous race or family to be demanding a sign.[1] But - and here is the helpful bit - "no sign would be given them except the sign of Jonah[2]".

Why do I say "helpful"? Simply because when they heard the news that the executed criminal Jesus of Nazareth had risen again, **they**

---

[1] I have no idea why "generation" is such a common translation in this verse and elsewhere; it is a relatively marginal meaning of the Greek word γένος - genos - and makes far less sense in the context than the core meaning of "race, clan, family or kin"

[2] Generally understood to be a reference to Jesus' resurrection after 3 days in the tomb, just as Jonah spent 3 days in the belly of the whale.

might see a sign they could finally understand; something which finally demonstrated to them that the coming of the Kingdom of God was not subject, at all, to **their** rules and expectations. They will in fact be given a sign, and it is the one sign they cannot misunderstand. Why do we see that as Jesus mocking them? He is showing them the kindness He can, given the circumstances.

And that brings us to the critical element underpinning both this passage, and the conversation with Nicodemus in John 3 (not to mention large swathes of the Gospels in general): **frame of reference.**

If you want to understand why Jesus seems hard, maybe even a little heartless at times, in some of His interactions with people, it is because He consistently refuses to say or do anything which could be misunderstood by them as accommodating a non-Kingdom frame of reference.

He would much rather leave people frustrated and asking "what am I not getting here?", than to set them on a false path. They needed to lose their old frame of reference if they were ever to develop a Kingdom mindset.

No one can receive the Kingdom as a kind of overlay upon their existing religious thinking. Including me and you.

Conversely, look at Jesus' interactions with non-Jews who do "get it". A Centurion asks Him to heal his servant; Jesus says He will come and heal him. The Centurion says "no, I wasn't asking you to rearrange your priorities for today - but I understand authority, so I was asking you to exercise authority on my servant's behalf." Jesus says of the Centurion "nowhere in all Israel have I found such faith." The Kingdom is about authority.

The Syro-Phoenician woman with a demonised daughter asks Jesus to heal her. Jesus rebuffs her with "It is not right to take the children's bread and give it to the little dogs." Her reply to Him is in effect, "Okay, so even if my daughter and I *were* little dogs, surely we would still get to eat the crumbs that fall under the table, right?" Or if you prefer, "Little dogs or not, I am claiming my place in your household."

The Kingdom is about provision and a household in which everyone is welcome (but which not everyone ever bothers to approach or enter). **That** is a Kingdom mindset.

Both the woman and the Centurion demonstrated to Jesus that they weren't invested in the religious system, but rather that they understood enough of the Kingdom He represented that they could ask for what they needed. There are many other examples - the blind men who cry out for mercy to the Son of David. "What do you want," Jesus asks. The religious answer would be "give us alms in our suffering". The Kingdom answer is, "we want to see"!

Back to our passage and we now have the backdrop to understand what Jesus says next, to the disciples in the boat. It is a command.

> *"Be on watch and hold fast against the leaven of the Pharisees and of Sadducees..."*
> **Matthew 16:6, my rendering**

What does Jesus have against leaven (yeast)? Well, nothing of course: the use here is metaphorical, and it is a specific yeast: "the yeast of the Pharisees" (Matthew, Mark, Luke) and "the yeast of the Sadducees" (Matthew) or "of Herod" (Mark).

When the disciples don't follow what he is saying, Jesus makes it clear that He refers to the teaching of the Pharisees and that of the

Sadducees or "of Herod".

A quick aside on "the leaven of Herod" in Mark's version, because it is a rather surprising idea.

No one amongst the disciples was likely to listen to Herod, let alone pay any attention to his teaching - even in the unlikely event that he did begin to teach. At least one of the earliest Papyrus copies of Mark has "Herodians" rather than Herod, which would make sense: as far as we can ascertain, "the Herodians" (i.e. the main political support and powerbase for Herod, apart from the Romans themselves) was almost synonymous with "the Sadducees"; these 'non-supernaturalists' ("who say there is no resurrection") used religion as the basis for the exercise of political power.

So the yeast of the Sadducees or Herodians might be precisely that: **teaching that used religion to achieve political ends.** All I will note is that Jesus said, "Beware!"

Now Jesus clearly has nothing against yeast itself, since He **also** uses yeast as a figure of the Kingdom of God. We will understand what He says about "the leaven of the Pharisees", only if we understand what He says about the Kingdom being like leaven, too.

"The kingdom of heaven is like yeast that a woman took and mixed into about sixty pounds of flour until it worked all through the dough."

(Matt 13:33, NIV, see also Luke 13:21)

We need to clear away our modern kitchen experience to see the whole picture here. For a start, this is wheat meal, rather than our modern fine flour. And the Greek simply says "until this was all leavened." No mention of dough, as such.

And that is because the process described is actually about turning the three *sata* (more like 45 pounds, actually) of wheat meal **into leaven**. (Not dough).

"Leaven" is a more accurate term than the 'yeast' of the NIV and other modern translations. Yeast - the fungus - is involved, but ζύμη (*"zumh"*) is technically leaven, which is not the little packet of dry yeast we would recognise, but rather "slightly damp, fungus-infected wheat meal". You can turn it into bread, or you can use it to make yet more leaven.

So Jesus is actually talking about a woman taking some previously made ζύμη or leaven, and hiding it in forty-five pounds of wheat meal until all of that wheat meal is leavened, i.e. it has all become ζύμη, or leaven, too.

This might be important. This is **not** a saying about how plain old flour becomes a big fluffy loaf of bread. (Flour + Yeast = Bread, hoorah...).

Instead, Jesus says "the Kingdom of God is like a woman hiding leaven in a big pile of flour **until it is all leaven**". At that point, she can take any portion of the pile, and it is all the same as the leaven she started with. So **it is actually a parable about increasing the supply of leaven**, not about making a bowl of dough from which to make bread.

Let's tease that out further, because it will help us understand the commandment in Matthew 16:6.

The little parable Jesus uses to explain the Kingdom in Matt 13:33 and Luke 13:21 is making some simple but powerful points:

1. The Kingdom is about multiplication (a small lump of leaven becomes 20kg of leaven; and what could **that** not become, in its turn?)

2. The process of the Kingdom is hidden (the woman hides the lump of leaven in the wheat meal, she doesn't put it on top in plain sight.)

3. The Kingdom multiplies by association and even "infection" (wheat meal becomes leaven by being in close proximity to leaven; the yeast involved "eats" wheat meal and ferments it, while also multiplying itself.)

Without pushing the parable too far, we can also conclude that the lump of leaven hidden in the flour is "Jesus modelling (demonstrating and explaining) the Kingdom". Flour (men and women) that lives in close association with the leaven (Jesus modelling the Kingdom) gets infected and becomes itself, more leaven (men and women who model the Kingdom).

It is a highly effective plan. Even the Sanhedrin would later testify to the effectiveness of this process:

> *When they saw the courage of Peter and John and realized that they were unschooled, ordinary men, they were astonished and* **they took note that these men had been with Jesus.**

> **(Acts 4:13, NIV, emphasis mine)**

This picture of the Kingdom and its operation is somewhat different to the average Christian's understanding and frame of reference.

Most believers are looking for deliverance, i.e. that Jesus would come and fix their marriage, pay their bills and end their hard labour.

The biblical picture we find in this parable is that we would become like Jesus, meaning that we would have exactly the same effect on other people as Jesus does. As we have seen in earlier chapters, that also means that we would exercise exactly the same power and authority that we see Jesus exercising, and in the same manner.

As a friend of mine says, "We don't wait for deliverance, we bring deliverance!"

If your reaction at this point is, "but I have tried to be like Jesus, and I just end up being more and more like me," then perhaps you weren't paying attention. You **will** be just like Jesus if you submit to the Kingdom process. 'Trying' plays no part: you need to be infected and changed by the Kingdom teaching of Jesus and by being with Him and His Kingdom disciples.

So, returning to the much ignored commandment about leaven, Jesus felt it was necessary to issue a significant warning. Although we have used mostly Matthew's version so far, let's look at a more literal rendering of the original Greek of *Mark's* version of the commandment, in Mark 8:15:

> *He gave express orders to them, saying*
> *"Look! Watch out [to be] free from*
> *the leaven of the Pharisees*
> *and the leaven of the Herodians*

In the past, I would have read this as a warning not to "take on board" aspects of Pharisaic or Herodian thinking[3], ideas that might infect us without our realising it when we are trying to follow Jesus.

But by now, you, like me, should be seeing a more profound threat.

> *If you hide a little lump of Pharisee leaven in a big pile of wheat meal, you will end up with **a whole big lump of Pharisee leaven**.*

Not only will the whole pile **be** Pharisees, but **everyone they touch**

---

[3] *For example, this passage comes to mind whenever I hear someone in Church telling us that "we must learn to read all the different levels of meaning in Scripture, just as the Jews of Jesus' day would have". As far as I can see, focusing on hidden layers of meaning is what the Pharisees (amongst others) did; and also, what Jesus **scrupulously** avoided doing on any and every occasion. (Jesus was constantly affirming that God's Word meant exactly what it said; and when He spoke "hidden things", they were hidden in plain sight; which hopefully this small book has helped you recognise.)*

will become Pharisees too. (Or Herodians / Sadducees, if you want to be accurate and comprehensive.)

I have already suggested above that Herodian leaven is teaching that uses religion for the pursuit of political power; Pharisaic leaven is teaching that uses religion for the pursuit of spiritual power.

In both cases, it is a) teaching which is b) using religion and c) aimed at achieving power **over others**. It is therefore about being and staying in control. (And "being in control" very easily becomes a 'good' in its own right; if you told a Pharisee that the Kingdom had no room for "people being in control of religious orthodoxy", they might well ask, "but what else is there?")

The Kingdom of God is about power too; but it is **power exercised under the authority of the King and for the benefit of others**. "But I am among you as one who serves," says Jesus (*Luke 22.27, NIV*).

So this is the express commandment of Jesus[4]. "Make sure you remain uncontaminated by teaching that will turn you into a Pharisee (someone in pursuit of religiously-framed spiritual power over others) or a Herodian / Sadducee (someone in pursuit of religiously-framed political power over others)."

Why does He issue this commandment? Because as I suggested earlier, there is no accommodation possible between the Kingdom of God (ruled by God) and those who want to be in control of a religious system, for whatever reason.

You can be the Leaven of the Kingdom; or you can be the Leaven

---

[4] The language of Mark 8:15 conveys the idea that Jesus is a supreme commander giving express orders in writing (διεστέλλετο) to his subordinates; the point of written orders being that in the case of failure to execute, the written order given can be used in evidence against you at your court-martial, usually with your life at stake on the outcome.

of the Pharisees and Sadducees. Whichever you are, **you will reproduce after your own kind**. You cannot be both.

What does this mean for me?

Well, first up, if you think there is any chance that the leaven against which Jesus warned His disciples has contaminated or shaped your thinking, then this could account for any difficulties you may be having in fully experiencing the Kingdom.

The truth is, that it can - **potentially** - take quite a long time to get free of that mindset, in order to see the Kingdom. The problem of course it this: **you cannot think your way out of a way of thinking**, and for the obvious reason - every thought can only be processed within the frame of reference you already have.

The good news is that the most ultra-Pharisee of all time became the most effective apostle of the Kingdom. He encountered Jesus on the road, and was so completely changed by the experience, that within days he was refuting his old allies in public. But he also apparently spent 14 years, out of sight in Arabia, before he was fully ready to fulfil his assignment from the Lord. (So don't run before you can walk this out.)

Now do you understand why Paul says "do not be conformed any longer to the template of this world, but be transformed by the renewing of your minds"? Something needs to be renewed. The Kingdom answer has always been the renewal of minds by seeing something of the King and His Kingdom. This means that the **modelling of the Kingdom** is super important. Words, alone - say, like this book - **don't come close**.

That is also why Paul says in 1 Corinthians 4:20 "... for the Kingdom of God is not in a hypothesis (or a theory or a word) but in the ability to do (or execute)." Now the NIV says "not in words but in power"; but that may be to miss what Paul was saying; facing people who were "putting him down" in his absence, he was saying that when he came to Corinth, he wouldn't be interested in what they had to say but what they could demonstrate of the Kingdom.

I don't think he was planning some kind of dramatic confrontation, which the NIV's "power" may seem to suggest, but rather looking for **the evidence** - healing, provision, situational wisdom, authority exercised over situations and spiritual powers - **that they were actually walking out the Kingdom**. And he already knew by their actions that he was unlikely to see that evidence.

So the reason this book is a provocation rather than a field manual is that to really "get the Kingdom", you will need to find people with whom to walk this all out. And that is true whether you are a Church leader, or a new believer, or even someone who thought they had given up on God altogether. Mental assent by itself gets you nowhere; we all need to be experiencing the Kingdom.

So, where to next?

Well, we are done for now, but one last thing, which may be an encouragement.

When Jesus issued His command about leaven, the disciples assumed it was a rebuke because they forgot to bring bread. He finally got them to understand that He was warning them to stay away from the teaching and thought-system of the nation's religious leaders. But in the process He underlined something very important for them.

In the Kingdom, bread is not an issue.

"Don't you remember the 5000 and how many baskets were left over? And the 4000, and how many buckets were left over? How do you not understand that bread isn't the issue here?"

In other words, even if your whole life up until this point has been the search for provision, or bound by the fear that somehow what you have will prove not to be enough, that is **not** your portion in the Kingdom.

Citizens of the Kingdom need to understand stuff, and they need to see their assignment; but as you learn the Kingdom, you will discover that wondering where your next meal or your next dollar is coming from - or fearing that it won't - is not part of the equation.

"Fear not, little flock, for the Father is pleased to give you the Kingdom!"

Afterword: Nowhere to lay His head

Jesus replied, "Foxes have dens and birds have nests, but the Son of Man has no place to lay his head."

(Matthew 8:20, NIV)

I closed the last chapter of this short book with the suggestion that the modelling of the Kingdom is critical. So before we get too carried away, we do need to ask ourselves, "but what did Jesus model for us Himself?" Surely He went about having and holding nothing of His own, and we wouldn't suggest He failed to fulfil His assignment.

Take the verse above. It seems clear enough: animals have homes, but Jesus doesn't. Although we would never say it this way, **it looks to us like Jesus is a homeless person**. Isn't that what He modelled for us?

Let's have a look. We need to go back to Matthew 4, first:

"When Jesus heard that John had been put in prison, he withdrew to Galilee. Leaving Nazareth, he went and lived in Capernaum, which was by the lake in the area of Zebulun and Naphtali"

(Matthew 4:12-13, NIV)

The Greek is a lot more definitive than the NIV. κατῴκησεν ("*katwkhsen*") is, most simply, 'settle in' or 'colonise', but always has a formal legal sense to it (it can also refer to non-citizens moving into a jurisdiction, or even to a person taking on the administration of a city or state). So Jesus left Nazareth and **settled in** Capernaum.

Where in Nazareth did He live before He moved?

Presumably in the family home, since He was the eldest son of the house, and responsible for His mother and unmarried siblings. When

He settled in Capernaum, did He bring His mother with him, or did she stay in Nazareth? We simply don't know for sure.

However, Mark 3:20 onwards gives us some reason to believe that His mother - and brothers - were probably living separately from Jesus, even if just in another house in Capernaum.

Firstly, despite what the NIV suggests ("Then Jesus entered a house..."), Καὶ ἔρχεται εἰς οἶκον just means "And He went home..." - in the sense of going into the house, where He lives.

Think for a moment. If you are out at the shops, and say to your spouse, "I need to pop back to the house", whose house are you going to pop back to? Your house, of course, unless you are on a trip and staying with someone, in which case you mean their house.

You **never** mean "I am going to pop into **a** house..." Not unless you are a cat burglar.

It is hard to avoid the sense that in any other context, Καὶ ἔρχεται εἰς οἶκον would be translated most simply and obviously as "He went home" or "He went to His house"; but because it is Jesus, **who mustn't have a house**, we bend over backwards to say something else.

Having got back to His place, crowds surround the house, and He and the disciples who stayed with Him didn't even get a chance to eat. **When His family heard this**, they came to take charge of Him, because they said that "He is deranged" (literally, "out of His place").

So - they were close enough to hear what was going on, and they knew where He was (they turned up outside His house); but they clearly weren't living in the house.

What **we can tell** is that **Jesus wasn't sleeping in the park**.

He bought a house, or rented part of a house or something else which amounted to "settling in Capernaum". Did it have His tools and a workshop attached? We don't know, but it is unlikely that He could have found a house with **no space** in which to carry on a business. That is not to say He used any workshop space He may have had for carpentry. But He had a house.

So what about His conversation, recorded in Matthew 8, with the teacher of the Law, who said he would follow Jesus wherever He went?

I don't think there is any reason to read Jesus' reply, in Matthew 8:20, as if it is saying that Jesus is now homeless. ("I was so busy preaching, I missed a mortgage payment..." No way!) Think about the **context**.

The teacher of the Law is making a statement, perhaps heart-felt, perhaps just for public consumption. "Wherever you go, I will follow..."

Jesus has just come back from addressing huge crowds on the hillside by the lake. On His way into Capernaum, He has healed a leper, healed the Centurion's servant, gone into Peter's house and healed His mother-in-law, and then healed all the demon-possessed brought to Him at the door of Peter's house when evening came.[1] Having driven out all the spirits with a word, Jesus has issued instructions to the disciples that they need to get away across the lake this evening. Why?

Because with the huge crowds from the hillside still in the neighbourhood, and growing all the time as locals are healed, if He tries staying at home in Capernaum, the whole thing will just get out of hand.

---

[1] *Please note: when He goes into someone else's house, we are told whose house; except that, as we shall see in a moment, sometimes the English translations make a bad guess that it was someone else's house. In this case it really was Peter's house.*

So what does He say to the teacher of the Law?

"The foxes have dens, and the birds of the heavens, roosts, but the Son of Man doesn't know where He should lay His head."

(Matthew 8:20, my rendering)

Firstly, the literal meaning of κατασκηνώσεις (*kataskhnwseis*) is "encampments"; it is definitely not nests. Jesus is picturing a tree full of birds roosting, not a solitary thrush on its lonely, personal nest. So "roosts" is as close as we can get in English without sounding odd.

Secondly, ἔχει (*exei*) in the phrase ὁ δὲ υἱὸς τοῦ ἀνθρώπου οὐκ ἔχει ποῦ τὴν κεφαλὴν κλίνῃ, and which the NIV translates as "the Son of Man **has** no place to lay his head", can be just as accurately rendered as "know" (ἔχω as possess mentally = know, understand; rather than just possess = have, hold). It could also be read as 'doesn't know **how** He will get His head down'

We already know the how and the where: the answer to His question is "in the back of the boat, at least until the disciples panic".

Jesus is **not saying "I'm homeless"**. He is saying "following me wherever I go? That may not be as much fun as you think. I'm tired, there's all these crowds meaning I can't just go home, and I don't know how I can get my head down for a few minutes this evening ... So tell me: is that what **you** are putting your hand up for?"

Perhaps you are not convinced yet.

Have a look at Matthew chapter 9. The first verse says that Jesus returned to His own town (NIV), or more literally "His own city". Capernaum is the city so referenced, and in both English and Greek the implication is the same: He lived as a (proper) resident of that city.

A few verses later, we read this:

*"While Jesus was having dinner **at Matthew's house**, many tax collectors and sinners came and ate with him and his disciples."*

(Matthew 9:10, NIV, emphasis mine)

The funny thing is that the Greek doesn't mention Matthew at all.[2] A literal rendering says:

"And leading [them = the disciples, implied] from that place, He saw a man sitting at the tax booth, called Matthew, and said to him, "Follow me."
And getting up, he followed Him. And it happened, Him reclining [i.e. for a meal] in the house, and see, many tax-farmers and sinners coming, they ate with Jesus and His disciples."

(Matthew 9:9-10, my literal rendering)

If I am leading a group of people along the street, and as I pass you I say "follow me" and you do so, whose house do we end up eating dinner in? You followed me, so you would be pretty surprised if you suddenly realise I have lead you - and a crowd - to your house for dinner.

Did it happen with Zacchaeus (Luke 19)? Yes. And Jesus said "come down Zacchaeus, I must stay at your house today." Not, "come down, and follow me to a surprise location: your house!" As far as we can tell, only Jesus went in with Zacchaeus. Not the crowd, certainly.

So, taking the text of Matthew 9 on its own merits, it seems more likely that they are at Jesus' house. It could, of course, be the house of one of the other disciples, previously arranged. Matthew's house

---

[2] *Καὶ ἐγένετο αὐτοῦ ἀνακειμένου ἐν τῇ οἰκίᾳ, καὶ ἰδοὺ πολλοὶ τελῶναι καὶ ἁμαρτωλοὶ ἐλθόντες συνανέκειντο τῷ Ἰησοῦ καὶ τοῖς μαθηταῖς αὐτοῦ. Spot the Matthew... And no, μαθηταῖς is "disciples"*

seems a very surprising option, given the context of "follow me", and in the absence of any conversation which would support "the Matthew's house option".

Before you ask, the NIV version of Mark 2:14 onwards has exactly the same (to my mind) unfounded assumption, in this case taking the Greek for "he reclined in his house" to mean that Jesus was reclining in Levi's house. Still no explanation of how "follow me" takes them to Levi's house - whether or not Levi is the same person as Matthew.

So why do we have such trouble with this? As far as we can tell, Rabbis then did as Rabbis do now, namely they owned or rented a large house or other meeting place where they could live and their followers could gather to them, or even live with them.

So when Andrew and the other disciple ask Jesus, "Rabbi, where are you staying?" in John 1, they are asking to come and stay with Him; they know He must have a place for disciples to gather around Him. (And the phrase covers "staying at home", "lodging" or just general "staying".)

If you read the beginning of Mark chapter 2, prior to the "Levi" passage, you see the same picture again and again. In verse one, "the people heard he had come home". Literally this passage reads "they heard that He was in [the] house". So "the people heard that He was at home", would be more correct, provided you understand this in the sense of "in His house", **not** just "back in Capernaum".

So when, a few verses later, the paralytic's friends remove the roof to lower him down, it is Jesus" roof they are removing. And yes, it says a great deal about Jesus' priorities (compared to ours) that the passage says "when Jesus saw their faith, He said 'son, your sins are forgiven'", instead of "when Jesus saw the hole in his roof, He shouted, 'Oi! Stop that...'"

The problem is, "Jesus with a house" offends us because that isn't the mental picture we have been living with our whole lives. Frankly, it is time we took that picture to the tip, metaphorically speaking.[3]

So if you have been worrying that, despite everything I have suggested, Jesus was a homeless man and living on a park bench or sofa surfing with His long suffering friends...

No. No He wasn't. He had a home.

Enjoy that Kingdom!

---

[3] And please don't leave it at the metaphorical charity shop: no one else needs to take home this illogical and distorted view of Jesus either.

Visit *seeingthekingdom.com* if you are interested to explore further.

Author Bio

Jonathan Mason has Masters Degrees from Trinity College, Cambridge (Theology) and from the Graduate School of Business, Northern Territory University (Development Management). He won the R.H.Lightfoot prize for Ecclesiastical History at Cambridge for his revisionist dissertation on *Le Cénacle de Meaux*, a group of Catholic Humanist Reformers in 16th Century France. The members of *le cénacle* had previously been regarded as closet Lutherans; for the most part they were in fact simply responding to what they read in the Gospels, a theme not unrelated to this current book. Jonathan worked in a variety of missional and business organisations before starting (with his wife Sarah) a business called Elaura in 2000, initially in the UK and then expanding to Singapore. Kokkoi is their newest venture, based in NZ, where they now live. Sarah and Jonathan have four adult children, in England, Wales, Western Australia and NZ.